Navestone

Harcar

Longstone

Wamses

Brownsman

Staple Island

Megstone

Crumstone

FARNE ISLANDS
(enlarged)

LY ISLAND

aw

Inner Farne

Budle Point

FARNE ISLANDS

Islestone

MBURGH

Monkshouse

Glororum

SEAHOUSES

Spindlestone

Snook

Annstead

Beadnell Harbour

Chathill

Beadnell Bay

ELLINGHAM

AM

NWICK

N

N·K

BETWEEN THE
MUCKLE CHEVIOT
AND THE SEA

BETWEEN THE MUCKLE CHEVIOT AND THE SEA

Echoes of a Northumbrian Family

David Hay

Drawings by Dennis Mallett, M.S.I.A.

Paul Harris Publishing

1975

First published 1975 by
PAUL HARRIS PUBLISHING,
50 Montrose Terrace, Edinburgh,
in an edition of 1,500 copies only

ISBN 0 904505 1

Printed by the Shetland Times Ltd., Lerwick, Shetland

TO THE HAY FAMILY

Not forgetting our Ewing cousins and ancestors without whom there would have been no family history!

Many of the local happenings which, we hope, will amuse a much wider audience of all those who enjoy Northumbria, would have been lost had they not been written down long ago by my Aunt Mabel Hay (Mrs Bell) and my cousins Jeanie and Charles Ewing; to them blessings and thanks. As will be seen from the text, I have leant heavily on the anecdotes of Grandmother Kate, gathered verbally, and upon the long memories and enduring wit of my Uncle John, my father and his two great school friends, Dr Joe Baker and Burdus Redford, at whose feet I sat as a small boy. I was completely enraptured by their stories of a Northumbria of long ago and a race of local characters long since dead. With their knowledge of Border legend and powers of reconstructing incident and personality no listener could have grown tired and I count myself among the lucky ones.

CONTENTS

LINE DRAWINGS

ILLUSTRATIONS

PREAMBLE

You will find no instruction in these pages nor even the vindication of a great cause or the inner history of the 19th century. But the men and women who come to life through the family history of one or two of the border clans on either side of the Cheviots may bring back to you memories of places and people that we both know well, like the old familiar tunes of the Beggar's Opera or the long forgotten Border Lays of old Northumbria.

CHAPTER I

BETWEEN THE MUCKLE CHEVIOT AND THE SEA

I have since discovered that I wasn't actually born in a coble. I only mention this, in passing, because a child's mind tends to be rather firmly dominated by his environment. Mine—at what the modern female psychiatrist might euphemistically call the dawn of earliest perception—was about as stable as a flea in a high wind; I was, I remember only too well, being very, very sick into the North Sea somewhere off St. Cuthbert's cell on the Farne Islands.

A coble may be a honey of a little fishing boat in the loving hands of a horny fisted old Northumbrian shell-back, but to a small boy of about four, in a rising seaway the motion is beyond belief. I was quite sure that the bottom had fallen out of the universe and the sun, which seemed to be loose in the sky, would soon fall into it.

This, in those halcyon days before the first World War, was my first conscious recollection of the family world of Border Legend and sea faring venture. The land where, when the Union put an end to official raiding, men and women with clan names like our own—the Hays and the Ewings and the Haigs—settled down to making perhaps a less exciting but more peaceful living from the moorland farms of Cheviot or from the restless sea that surges up and down that bleak coastline.

The area covered by the family papers is no more than that small triangle of Cheviot hill country bounded by Ettrick Forest and the Tweed on the Scottish side and the North Sea from Beadnell Bay to Berwick along the narrow coastline plain on the English side. To the rest of England, it long remained an outland place of grim border castles looking out across wind swept moorlands and back over a wreck strewn coast. After all was it not

North of the Roman Wall and all that that symbol of law and order meant. But to us, from our earliest moments of nostalgic memory, it was enchanted ground and the scene of ancient wars. It was the land not only of forays and knightly deeds, it was also the land of 'the little people' and the Laidly Worm of Spindleston Heugh. The little village of Bamburgh under its great castle on the basalt rock had been the first capital of all the land North of the Humber and more powerful than any other Saxon kingdom. But there were also Celtic pockets in the hills as the names of farms recall, pockets which survived the coming of the dour Friesland peoples from Schleswig in the days after the Romans went home and the border stock is the more imaginative for their being.

When you come to think of it, Cheviot itself is Celtic, so are Tweed and Tyne, not to mention many a town and village like Lindisfarne, Jarrow and Amble. The next door village went by the intriguing name of Glororum but no place name book has any suggestions to offer as to its origin. My Nanny used to say it was a contraction of Glower o'er 'em and who am I to gainsay such a one.

It is a land where every window commands great distances, across to the Farne Islands at sea, or landwards to where the Cheviots lie piled up against the frontier horizon. And a frontier horizon it was, until the union of 1707, with all the robust characteristics which are inevitable in a province between two countries. So, romantic as this breezy spacious upland country was, it was a robust romance with few illusions of gentleness in its human relations but for all that, the poets and the border minstrels, from the village bard to Sir Walter Scott, never lost sight of the gentler matters of the spirit and in their songs you will find the scent of flowers and of moorland heather and you will never be far from the sound of the waterfalls. The moorland farms and coastal cottages may have lacked the rose girt, ivy ringed, mellow old age of the South country but they had their moments of autumn sunshine and were at one with their land of origin.

People one talks to, invariably remember that Northumbria gave birth to Ida the Flame bearer and leaders like Harry Hotspur or Captain John Smith, the slayer of Turks and founder of Virginia who was wrecked on Holy Island. But they are apt to forget her gentle sons who left a far more enduring legacy than all the warrior kings lumped together; that gentle schoolman Duns Scotus, or St. Aidan, that unbelievable mixture of saintliness and administrator who brought off the miracle of turning this rough, bloodthirsty corner of borderland to Ionian Christianity in his lifetime, to become the first Bishop of a united Northumbria. In modern times one thinks of Grey of Fallodon watching his water birds. And may I add my own favourite character, St. Cuthbert, that Cheviot shepherd turned priest, who took over from St. Aidan and lived alone for years at a time on a remote Farne Island, caring for his own flock of sheep until he felt spiritually ready for his great task—more of him anon. It is a great pity that border warfare is always more attractive to the journalist than peaceful co-existence which never seems worth reporting.

My great grandfather, who was certainly no saint, also started life as a Tweedside shepherd on the same hillsides as St. Cuthbert. Though he was indeed a very respected elder of the Presbyterian Kirk, he left his moorland sheep eventually to make a living from the sea and in the every day account of his ventures into the chancy business of making a living in those early days of the Napoleonic wars and early industrial changes, we have perhaps as good a picture of this legendary border land as we are likely to get. At least it has the human and factual authority that is so often missing in the best reconstruction of a past century by historians, however diligent.

You will not find any of this family of ordinary people in your local history books but without them and thousands of borderers like them, there would have been no local history—for all the romantic or warlike posturing of those who 'made it' into the national lime light. On this unforgiving coast, you were lucky if you were allowed more than one mistake, and, indeed, quite a number of my own family hit one or other of the 28 Farne Islands on various dark nights of gale and rain and left only bits of wreckage for posterity to collect. But others survived and from their recorded doings we can get a fair idea of life in Georgian and Victorian times especially in the Bamburgh and Sea Houses area that lies between Berwick and Beadnall Bay.

Great grandfather Alexander was, according to his daughter's subsequent notes, about 14 and already a competent shepherd when his father, James Ewing, died in 1799 at the relatively early age of 55. James had farmed Fishwick Mains, which lies on the banks of Tweed below Ladykirk, all his life and was buried in the little Scottish Kirk of Fishwick a mile away to the North. This is the

Norham Castle still looks across the Tweed
to Fishwick Mains and Ladykirk

heart of the debateable land, on the Scottish side of the border between the Cheviots and the Lammermuir hills; it is indeed the land of fairies, forays and long forgotten battles. Shallow glens wind away up into the green hills and woods, beloved of Sir Walter Scott in his later years, with their legendary Peel towers and fortified farm houses in the clearings and wandering trout streams, like the Whiteadder that I knew so well as a boy.

Further up, past the beautiful ruins of Fairnilee (surely a fit abode for the queen of the fairies) the river winds past the tower of Elibank, Inner Leithen and Traquair House and on up the Teviot to Hawick where my grandfather lived before he 'went foreign' and crossed the Cheviots into Bambro' to wed my grandmother. There the wooded hills and the great abbeys of Melrose and Jedburgh give place to the rolling fastnesses of Ettrich and and Moffatdale. But it is, surely, the lower reaches of the Tweed that are the great farming lands of the Border Country and especially of sheep farming.

Now, in the autumn of 1799, the great stone house of Fishwick Mains overlooking the Tweed is unusually quiet, after the funeral procession has left. The barns stand full of a good year's crops and the autumn sheep dipping has just been finished. In the days that follow, son Alexander carries on philosophically with his herding and learns to take his place among the older hands at the drover's fair. His uncle takes over the farm and the valley of Tweed once more pursues its even tenor, commenting now and then in a detached sort of way on Napoleon's Egyptian campaign as it was reported in the local paper or looking curiously at drawings of Mr Robert's airships which were, not too successfully being developed in the North of France.

Alexander was content, for the moment, with the sun and the wind in summer and the snows and biting sleet of winter that go to make up the life of a hill shepherd. Sometimes, when digging maggots out of the bleeding backsides of half dead sheep with fingers frozen by the cold and drenched to the skin with the unending rain, he would wonder if there might not be a slightly more intelligent way of earning bread and butter. But with that determination to become good at the job in hand, that was later to make him a perfectionist in his own somewhat self-willed way, we find him still busy shepherding, seven years later when he is just twenty-one.

Of the hill country and of his companions, the Border shepherds, I can at least speak with personal knowledge—albeit about a century later—because, on comparing notes and family reminiscences I find that in spite of the industrial revolution elsewhere in England and wars and developments abroad, nothing much seems to have happened to change the shepherd's way of life between 1800 and the early years of the twentieth century.

It is hard to think of a more instinctive camaraderie than that of the Border shepherds even as they were when I was a boy. Then, I used to be up before dawn so I could be away with them to visit distant hills for collecting or lambing and many's the night I spent in the shelter of an intack round a heather fire, snug from the wind and open to the stars. They were men of the long stride and tireless step, clear eyed and with the slow smile of hillmen and the lilting speech of the Borderer.

Often, of a Sunday I have known them take their dogs with them to church. Once settled into the pews, the animals would sit quietly enough—until the blessing, when everybody stood up. This, they soon got to know was the joyful signal that the time to scamper out was near. To obviate this the congregation used to remain quietly seated during the blessing. This completely threw one visiting preacher who stood, waiting for his congregation to rise, until an old shepherd said in a loud voice,

'Say awa' minister; we're a' sittin' just to cheat the dowgs.'

I remember also, there was still good trout to be had

in the moorland burns and after some false starts I became quite an expert 'guddler.' Well known though this sport would be to Alexander, it was unknown in the South and I suppose, to modern youth anywhere, with his gallery of rods and nets and other sophisticated equipment. In those days, we only had our hands and feet but we learnt to use them to good effect. The art was to enter the peat brown water, rather like an old heron, making little movement as one edged towards some likely stones or undercut bank where the trout would love to lie, head up stream, waiting for tasty grubs and insects. Then you would slide your hand in, almost imperceptibly, and feel along under overhanging stones literally inch by inch. The first touch of the trout's belly was the all important point, it had to be imperceptible and caressing. After that, given what seemed at the time almost infinite patience, things got easier. A trout loves to be stroked, just like any other creature and gets quite mesmerised, so that once he was semi-hypnotised by the enjoyment you could whip him out onto the bank with a quick flick of the wrist—and many a grazed knuckle I had in the doing of it! When one or two, generally rather small trout, had been achieved, then would come the great moment of lighting a wood fire and grilling them on the spot.

In the country of one's youth you can never be alone; there are too many friendly little ghosts round each corner to keep you company part of the way.

During the journey, half forgotten incidents and old tales come to mind. Many will recall Mr Gladstone who once said to a Tweedside shepherd, when a snow storm was imminent and he saw the sheep moving to higher land where the drifts would not lie,

'Are not sheep the most foolish of animals, if I were a sheep I would stay in the hollows.'

To which the shepherd replied simply,

'Sir, if you were a sheep you would have mair sense.'

And John Buchan once said, as far as I can remember

it, that the shepherds had two qualities he most admired, 'realism coloured by poetry' and 'a stalwart independence sweetened by courtesy' as well as a 'shrewd kindly wisdom.'

He recalls how at a lamb fair, one of his constituents just before an election paid him a somewhat left-handed compliment,

'We've gotten the richt sort of candidate in you this time. Your predecessor was an awfu' nice man but he was far ower much of a gentleman and far ower honest!'

It is, indeed this wonderful North Country use of the word 'honest' which is quite delicious. You will remember the old saying, (after someone had blamed Satanic influences for his own personal shortcomings),

'Indeed, the deil, honest man, has had ower mony things laid to his charge.'

But above all others, this is the land of Sir Walter Scott whose romances we delighted in since early memories of being read aloud to at bedtime. I don't think I really appreciated him fully until later life. Though I grew in the age that regarded him as outmoded, I was quite sure from the start that he was the prince of story tellers and I knew of no other who could hold a candle to him for that. Perhaps this was partly because he told of the country we were brought up in as children. Later on, of course, I came to reflect on his real worth and understood, more fully, the source of his appeal. I still think it is the simple genuineness and wholesome nature of his approach to life that is his abiding magnetism. I can't help feeling that too many modern critics, nurtured in an age of emotional insecurity have confused normality at its most refined peak, with mediocrity. He was the centre of his universe, a social being who saw the past from the grandstand of the present. He could combine a subtle sense of humour, a truly Chaucerian scale of merriment, with a delicate but sure understanding of the dark patches of the human character.

I like him because he had, as someone has said, 'a

kindly affection for the commonplace.' He had his faults but they were what made him so delightfully human. Witness the gross elaboration of the Abbotsford dream, or the fact that he never had time to tidy up either his prose or his plots, but his art never became artificial, it was too closely drawn from the bustling life around him and his prose came, like himself, of fighting stock. As he expressed it, 'the simplest soldier who carries a gun for his country is a sounder fellow than I am,'—but because he was on the same wavelength as his humblest characters, he understood them in a way few modern novelists seem able to do. His characters were all his friends and he merely led them back into the past and set them problems to solve and devised situations that would bring out their most attractive or typical characteristics.

Above all he knew his native land better than any one before or since. His legal work had taken him into every nook and cranny of the national character and across every historic landscape with its battle legends, squalid treachery and breathtaking poetry. Porters, merchants, caddies, tinkers, shepherds, judges, lairds and village dominies jostle for a place in his reconstructions of the market place he loved. The strife is seen through the window of sanity. Indeed I cannot escape the feeling, when I am regarding Scott, that we are both sitting at a window, warm and lit by the log fire and curtained by thick walls, while outside the storm rages and characters do battle, in a landscape which stretches beyond the horizon of both time and place. He never loses his grip of the scene and when we draw the curtains there is that inevitable feeling that our own life has been renewed by fresh and happier values — a feeling one gets only after reading Stevenson at his best or Shakespeare himself. Not even the twentieth century clever boys have denied that he was a 'master of clear, swift narrative prose!' What they mean is that he could tell a story superbly; and what more can you ask of a spinner of magical yarns?

B

The astonishing thing about the Border country, both Sir Walter's side and the Northumbrian is that it doesn't really matter whether you fall into an armchair and read him or walk across the moors today—nothing seems to have changed.

There are the same ancient hedges, bent almost at a right angle by the onshore gales, the same clouds of whaups and haycocks weighing a ton apiece and little trout streams wandering down from the moors across the upland pastures. Of course, haymaking is not the careful tidy process it is in the South, it is too wet for that. The great heavy pikes (cocks) are eventually loaded on a sort of sledge called a bogie and hauled over the rough ground to the farmstead for silage.

And so, I could paint, on the slightest excuse, a much fuller picture but it had better take shape in the most natural way of all, from the doings of the men and women who made up the actual people of the 'market place' at the time.

'If you haven't yet come under the spell of the country, I hope the last few pages will at least have given you a faint flavour of its magic. Forgive me if you feel I have lingered a little unduly over Sir Walter—as you may have gathered I rather enjoy him—but there was a deeper purpose. He was almost exactly a contemporary of Alexander Ewing the shepherd boy of Tweedside to whom I have already introduced you and whose recorded doings are going to carry us through the first sixty years of the 19th century in this corner of Northumbria—and, I thought, what better introduction could we have than the greatest of Border minstrels.

CHAPTER II

RAM TAM, MIDDLE BREW AND PINKIE

It is already the year 1806 and Alexander has celebrated his twenty-first birthday, to no mean tune by all accounts, for by this time his reputation as a fighter and wrestler (Northumberland style) at county fairs had spread throughout the border county. 'Short, broad, and strong beyond the ordinary,' was his daughter's description in later years, 'with pale blue eyes, one of which was sightless owing to an injury when he was a lad.' This was a direct result of his impetuous habit of taking on all comers to the ring at the annual county gatherings and sheep dog trials.

But, one gathers he was even more popular in the bar parlours afterwards, just as he had been on cold nights round the log fire in many a winter sheep fold, for he had a peculiarly deep rich voice and a growing repertoire of religious songs and folk music—the former being his first love.

By this time, however, he was becoming restless and the urge to branch out and become his own master and to try his hand at new and exciting trades had already broken his automatic acceptance of the steady round of the seasons that had been all-satisfying to his father at the Mains. The shepherd's sky between the hills at dawn or at the going of the light was no longer sufficient compensation for long nights of cold and wet with little profit or prospect of change.

He gets in touch with his elder brother Andrew and, farewells said, off they go to Horncliffe (which you will find nearby on the map) to learn the art of coopering. There was, in the early years of the Napoleonic wars, a great shortage of skilled coopers. Even in normal times of peace, barrels were in great demand, not only for beer but for the great and growing industry of fish curing on the East coast and for a host of other liquids and material that had to be kept in good condition for long periods because of the relative slowness of transport. The war and

Wrestling at a border country fair
(from a contemporary engraving)

demands of a greatly enlarged navy had intensified the need for barrels for pork, salt meat, drinking water and a hundred other necessities for ships on long passages or spells of station keeping on blockade duties.

The acquisition of the skill was probably looked upon as a sort of insurance, something to fall back on if other ventures failed—or it may have been the first thing that came to hand—I don't know. Certain it was that, across the border in Northumbria, no one could be out of a job as long as Ram Tam, Middle Brew and Pinkie were being brewed and drunk by fisherfolk at the Bamburgh Inn and many another up and down the coast. And speaking of the Bamburgh Inn, it was in 1800 owned by the father of a young lady who was eventually to become Alexander's wife; though not for many a long year yet.

Anyway, the two brothers were not exactly letting the grass grow under their feet. As soon as they could cooper a pretty barrel to everyone's satisfaction and thus have a safe trade to fall back on, they set off, over the border and made their way down to Alnwick, at that time a thriving market town. This must have looked a good spot in which to try their hands at setting up in business on their own. No, not making barrels or even filling them. They have heard that London is becoming so large and thriving that there isn't enough fresh farm produce in the home counties to satisfy the demand of society during the fashionable season. So they arrange to buy up large quantities of butter, eggs, bacon and general produce from the farms that used to send in to the market in Alnwick. The farmers are only too pleased to sell their goods in advance for a guaranteed price. They have to be got to London very quickly while they are fresh, much more quickly than the rough and uncertain state of the roads will allow. In any case there would have been no profit by road as the charges were prohibitively high.

By sea is the only sure—or reasonably sure—way of getting perishible goods to London at a cost that will leave a pleasant margin of profit for the merchant. So what do they do, but acquire or charter a few small clippers and man them with amateur crews from among their own friends in Berwick. It is a sporting and imaginative venture but I'm afraid it doesn't make a fortune for them for, within a year or two, Alexander has used up his savings and more and is forced to sell out and take another job while he pays off debts to friends and puts by enough to have another shot at an independent business. This time it is a job with a fish curing business at Eyemouth, a little town in his native county just North of Berwick.

Alexander, apparently, had too much drive and initiative to stay long as an assistant in Eyemouth and we find him suggesting that he should launch out on the firm's behalf and set up a new branch in Sea Houses. This busy little fishing harbour lies six or seven miles South of Lindisfarne (Holy Island) and four miles along the coast beyond Bamburgh the ancient capital. It almost dries out at low water but a large fleet of skaffies, fifies and Yorkshire type Billyboys were based there and for another hundred years the great shoals of herring were to bring growing wealth to the otherwise bleak Northumbrian coast.

The young Alexander worked hard, lived simply, paid off his debts and started putting money by again, with an eye to a second attempt at creating a business of his own. This time, though, it will be something within his own experience and competence; indeed what better prospects were there than in his present trade of fish curing. At present it was centred round Berwick and the Scottish side of the border but it could become just as firmly rooted on the Northumbrian side. His Eyemouth firm is obviously having similar ideas so there is no time to be lost if he is to get in first.

Hence we find him setting up on his own in Sea Houses where he can cash in on the great catches of herring coming in not only to that harbour but several other smaller but busy little harbours like Beadnell two miles to the South. No more depending on the fashionable and chancy whims of London society. Here was a field of activity he thoroughly understood and it would be based in a countryside he knew and could depend on.

So it was to the fish curing business that he turned his almost inexhaustible energies and not inconsiderable abilities. Money was the great problem, in spite of his careful savings during the last few years. There was no question of buying suitable premises let alone the equipment necessary to go with them. So he bought a piece of land near the harbour, up on the cliff and set to work with his own hands to build a 'yard' and equip it with rudimentary smoking and packing facilities.

He had two pieces of luck. First, Sea Houses didn't really exist as a separate entity yet, on any map. It was still the harbour for the little fishing village of Sunderland — elsewhere known as North Sunderland to avoid confusion with the large industrial port further South— about a mile inland. There were already a number of fishermen's houses down round the harbour which was becoming known locally as Sea Houses not to mention two chapels but land was still cheap and fairly easy to come by. So perhaps his timing was good judgment rather than luck.

The second piece of luck, however, was providential. His brother James, a bachelor, died about this time and left both Alexander and Andrew £300 each — a useful sum of money in 1828. This was a great help in buying materials and even employing a certain amount of labour to build the first smoke house, especially when brother Andrew decided to join the venture and add his savings to it. He doesn't seem to have taken a very active part in building up the business but any help at this stage would have been very welcome. Alexander had been wise enough to bring his old cooper, Will Spears with him. Will was not only to make his mark on the countryside as a whole but was to have a profound influence on the young Alexander himself. Possessed of almost inhuman energy, Alexander worked all hours of the day and often far into the night building the essential sheds and equipping them. He fished when time allowed, for food.

In order to put by enough money to plough into the yard and its new buildings more quickly, he lived alone in a cottage which was, in my young days, a smoke house. He seems to have lived extremely simply, mostly using his own barrels as dining room furniture. When the weather permitted, he and old Spears would walk down to the little harbour as soon as there was enough water to float the coble, and up would go the little sail as they squared away to the Farne Islands, dropping anchor in the 'kettle' if it was rough until such time as the stone breakwater was possible for loading. They brought back cobble stones with which they laboriously paved the under yard with their own hands.

On this coast everybody was a seaman, ready to put to sea at any time to help a ship in trouble. The lighthouse keeper on the Farnes, for example, records: —
March 6th. 'Storm S by E.

> The brig *Bravo* of Newcastle, coal laden, being in a leaky state was run on Balmbro sands and immediately filled. The crew took to the rigging and were taken off by the Balmbro boat manned by Wm Spears (Herring Curer) Robert Patrick (fisherman) Wm Berry (Coast guard) George Wilson (mason) and 3 mariners.

> The salmon fish boat also went to them but was blown off (course) to Berwick where they arrived safe, but much exhausted.'

As you will see on any chart or map, the Farne Islands dominate the coastline opposite Bamburgh Castle. They are about two and a half miles from Sea Houses harbour and number fifteen at high tide and twenty eight at low. I have mentioned them earlier and shall come back to my own recollection and the St. Cuthbert legends later on. But in the 18th century, so many ships were lost on them (thirty between 1756 and 76) with great loss of life that two light houses were built, at first coal burning and later oil lit. The lighthouse keepers were the well known Darling family. William took over from his father Robert as Head Keeper in 1815, and his famous Journal also adds a great deal to our feel of the flavour of life in this North East corner between this year and his retirement in 1860. He died at the Wyndings, Bamburgh in 1865 — four years before Alexander. I have a presentation copy in front of me as I write and will give you a few quotes because it is not just the log of wrecks and gales and all that goes to make up the daily round of a lighthouse keeper, but

it was a very human document and told of the visits of
fishermen and officials and domestic problems with the
boiler and attempts at growing vegetables and even flowers
on those wind swept rocks.

Above all, like my Aunt May (Mrs William King)
to whom a copy is presented by his son George in fair
copper plate writing of the period, William Darling was
a naturalist and bird watcher of no mean ability and his
diary of Farne Island birds and unusual arrivals and nest-
ings is a treasured record. William King was a son of
the harbourmaster at Sea Houses and both he and his
brother and sister (Great Aunt Anne as I knew her) were
close friends of the Darlings and similarly knowledgeable

Presented

To Mrs W. King

by George. A. Darling

Sea Houses

Decr 26th 1898

The only surviving brother

of Grace H. Darling

Longstone Lighthouse

Farne Islands

about the wild life. They make, naturally enough, many appearances in the Journal. In fact I suppose it was the two aunts, who by recalling, to a small boy, all the warm personalities and sights and sounds of those days, really gave this coast a depth and perspective for me in later life.

Aunt Anne, besides being a most amusing character when I knew her, in her eighties, drew beautifully and constructed wooden and cardboard animals of great character. The sea provided the Darlings and the Kings with both a turbulent living and an abiding relaxation— as the journal shows in the recording and study of the many birds that nested or stayed awhile during gales, or perhaps flew into the light on wild nights. The sea took Annie King's man early in life before they even had a chance to get married but it gave her back something in exchange — a sort of self reliance and acceptance of fate as part of a well ordered universe. Poor sweetie, the choice for sailors' wives or girl friends on that coast was the evolution of some sort of philosophy or of quietly going nuts. And so if you haven't read it, you will find, agreeably enough, that William Darling's Log was not always of gale, wreck and life saving, it contained also painstaking and accurate accounts of the birds which are now of great interest. But it is the human touches that stick in my mind as I re-read it today, for instance,

1830 April 6th 'I shot three Egyptian Geese and sent a pair to Newcastle Museum, the other to Mr Selby Tweizle House.'

June 24. 'The Tender at Longstone. George Beal cleaning the flues of the Wharf house boiler.'

or Nov. 24 'Gale East: Roof of Barracks broken in by the sea.'

or July 7. 'This evening remarkable darkness with continued rain, followed by whole gale E.N.E. veering N. lighted 30 minutes before sunset.'

or June 16. 'A Hurricane veering from W by S to NW almost totally destroying our gardens.'

March 29 'Wind W, Blowing fresh, schooner *Jemima* of Arbroath to Newcastle with sleepers, struck Knavestone Rock and at 1.30 I observed his signal light. We immediately launched our boat and with old Swan proceeded to the rescue and found her hanging by the head on the rock. Tide falling, she soon slid off,

William Darling
(from a contemporary engraving)

leaky but so the pump would keep her. Made shift to steer her by the sails for some hours.'

(A magnificent effort, reading between the lines of understatement — but today I fear his trades union would have merely fired him for over- stepping his duty).

Aug. 18 'Caught five barrels (of herrings) in the Hopper North Gut. Sold to G. Beal at 5/- a barrel.'

July 19. 'The *Pegasus* steamer struck Goldstone Rock
about 0.30 hrs and sank soon afterward with sixty
persons. Of these only 6 were saved by the *Martello*.'
In May of 1841 he must have had much pleasure
in recording,
'Messrs Walker and Burgers to plan W.B.D.'s house'—
a house for his son William Brooks who has been
appointed assistant keeper.
On Oct. 18 he records 'I and daughter E.G. (Elizabeth
Grace) caught the following birds, mostly on the
lantern.' There follows a long list including 34 Red-
wings and 22 Blackbirds.
April 1. 'Tremendous gales W. with snow showers. The
garden small seeds being all above ground were totally
blown off.'
Another entry reads, 'Between 5 and 6 a.m. high water,
the sea passed through the new building and filled
the new middle tank in the yard.'
Perhaps the nicest entry is a straight mistake of his
own which a lesser man might have been inclined to
omit. But in the same matter of fact language as the rest
of the log (August 20th 1843) it reads:
'About 10 a.m. W. B. Darling alone in the new boat
(a coble) got capsized in a squall, distant three miles
South from the Longstone; but getting on her bottom
was providentially rescued by Capt. James and his
men of the sloop *Shamrock* of Berwick-on-Tweed.'
Of course he has a magnificent view of the coast and
the Cheviots to which he several times refers, e.g.
Dec. 6. 'The hills and high land all covered with snow.'
On Sept. 23 he had written,
'Took up the last of Brownsman (on outer Farne)
potatoes this year, being a superior crop in quantity
and quality ever remembered here.'
Battles like Balaclava and Inkerman (with great
slaughter) find their way into the log, next door to 'The
Tailor at Longstone measuring for clothes.' 'Mr King'

comes at various times 'for barometer observations' on April 20th or 'to set George Beal to paving the jetty or North Road,' and his brother comes in December perhaps most welcome of all! — log reads 'Paid 24th by S. King.'

As you will probably remember, even the famous Grace Darling episode when he was assisted by his daughter in the rescue of survivors in the *Forfarshire*— with all its extravagant and quite impossibly romantic accounts in the London papers of Grace's having heard cries in the storm half a mile away against a head wind of gale force — appears thus in his own log:

'About 4 a.m. on the 7th the vessel struck the West point of Harker's rock and in fifteen minutes broke through by the paddle axe and drowned 43 persons . . . . nine others held on by the wreck and were rescued by the Darlings.'

Even when the secretary of Trinity House demanded a slightly less terse account he merely wrote: —

'7th Sept: it blowing a gale with rain from the North, my daughter and me being both on the alert before high water securing things out of doors, one quarter before five, my daughter observed a vessel on the Harker's rock but owing to the darkness and spray going over her could not observe any person on the wreck . . . until near 7 o'clock when 3 or 4 men were observed upon the rock. We agreed that if we could get near to them some of them could assist us back, without which we could not return. We immediately launched our boat (with the help of his wife Thomasin) and were enabled to gain the rock where we found eight men and one woman, which I judged rather too many to take at once so we took the woman and four men to the Longstone.'

Not many frills in that. They had to feed and accommodate the rescued crew members two days and nights until the full gale abated and a boat could put out for Sea Houses.

Now we had better go back to the mainland again, where by 1832 Alexander's fish curing establishment was humming and orders for cured fish of all sorts were coming in from a very wide area. This was to last for nearly a hundred years and provide welcome employment for a considerable number of local people.

To me, as a very small boy eighty years later, the great caverns of smoke filled halls with their racks of fish hanging in serried rows, had a magical quality not at all in keeping with the strictly commercial object of the establishment. Certainly the results were the most delicious things I have ever tasted. In those days there was no chemical dying or artificial methods. It was good oak sawdust smoke like the hams in the great chimney of the home farm at Mayfield where the aunts lived — Watties Row it was called in the early part of the century.

Will Spears seems to have been a bit of a character in his own right. Not only was Alexander persuaded to live with the Spears family during the cholera scare of 1832 but Will seems to have set about persuading him that there wasn't much future in a 'lonely bachelor's life' especially as Alexander had been busy building, in his spare moments, a pleasant house not far from the harbour. Will seems to have persuaded him that he would 'rattle about a bit' in a big empty house on his own and to have suggested marriage as a possible solution. Alexander is recorded as replying,

'Well, I don't suppose anybody would have me.'

But Will Spears was not to be put off so easily; he further suggested that Miss Isabella Saunders should be asked! And she was, and she said 'Yes' and they were married and went to live in the new house which was almost finished. They called it Horncliffe to commemorate the scene of his first venture away from his native hills after he had hung up his shepherd's crook for the last time. This was in 1832 and the house was still there when I last passed up the coast. Again, the sea had dominated

Isabella's childhood. Her father was the captain and owner of an East Coast Brig called, as far as we know, the *Anchor and Hope*. Anyway he traded from North Sunderland (Sea Houses was still not officially on the map) to the Tay, calling at harbours on the Forth if cargoes warranted it. Rather more to the point, however, he also owned the Bamburgh Castle Inn which, I imagine was even more profitable and certainly more fun than standing off the Northumbrian coast in an onshore gale.

It is a pity we haven't time to say much about his wife's mother, the sea captain's wife, because she was, I gather, a formidable character from Beadnell, (the only harbour on the East Coast to face West) and before that from Durham. Being used to a slightly more gracious and sheltered existence, the combination of seafaring and village inn came as a bit of a sudden eye opener to life but she squared up to it in no uncertain way, though the country folk continued to refer to her affectionately as Dame Saunders until her death.

But it was Isabella, her daughter, who revolutionised Alexander's life and the Yard itself, and must have shaken Sea Houses and North Sunderland to the wick. She must have had a natural gift for management for, without any training, she re-organised the methods of book-keeping and very soon became virtually the general overseer or manager of the factory. She seems to have gone through all departments like a dose of salts because she didn't in the least confine herself to the office block. Time and again if she scented trouble or sensed a falling off in production, she would slip on her pattens (clogs) and work along with the other women in the gutting, smoking or packing sheds. The local estimate in the 1830's was that she 'managed the women magnificent!'

I remember, years afterwards, seeing her account books which she always made herself, not only to save expense but because she liked them that way; beautifully neat ruled foolscap sheets bound together with twine and glue and sewn in to paste board covers.

One almost wonders why! Because she certainly didn't need them because of defective memory, as she knew exactly what came in and went out without ledger, daybook or railway book. In her day all the herring were smoked for red herring. There were no kippers or salted herrings for export to the continent or even pickled herrings such as those sent to Holland by the Lowestoft yards. About the first thing she discovered was that all the broken herrings were being thrown away — not even being used as manure. She soon put a stop to that and had them cured like the good ones and sold off at a cheaper rate. The proceeds went into her private account, one gathers, for dress allowance and social commitments because hard as she was worked, she was a gay person and could play hard as well.

They must have been an odd couple because they were almost exact opposites and Alexander was nineteen years older. Isabella was the life and soul of both villages. Indeed, Horncliffe soon became well known in the country-side round, for its parties and general kindly hospitality, especially to seamen temporarily without a ship or a shore job. And all this in spite of the fact that Alexander hated parties — at least he hated the noise and geffuffle they occasioned in the home, especially when he had been working late or had had a long session at the chapel of which he was an elder.

This happened more than once, because Isabella soon found it saved a lot of argument if she sent out invitations during his absence and preferably for nights when he would be away at Belford or Bamburgh. This worked most times but was apt to be less popular when he came home early, unexpectedly, for a meal and a quiet read by the fire. Even physically they were about as dissimilar as you could have arranged. Isabella was strikingly tall, dark haired and fair skinned, with a flair for gaily coloured dresses which she wore, as soon as she got away from the yard in the evenings, with panache and full blooded abandon.

Alexander, as already mentioned and as my grandmother (his daughter Kate) used to say was 'short, strong and bull necked with pale blue eyes and fair hair.' Only one eye was any good, owing to an injury when shepherding as a boy, together with a shoulder and various other injuries not only due to a rough and tumble sort of life but because he was, as his daughter described him, 'very impetuous, hot tempered and easily excited,' — the Scottish shepherd boy's reputation as a fighter and wrestler died hard.

He was a staunch Presbyterian and, like so many Borderers of that time, a bit dour with it. I don't really think he really ever accepted the fact that there might be some modicum of good, lurking at the back of another denomination. According to a well known quote, he was apt to regard protagonists of other forms of the faith as the Almighty might regard some particularly self willed black beetles.

For all that and his reputation of being a bit stern with his own children, he was trusted and loved in Sea Houses as a just man to his own work people and when appealed to in village matters. Many families were to stay with the firm for three generations.

Above all, he had what the Scots call "innerliness,' a quality found among hill folk, a compound of direct but homely simplicity with an emotional warmth which now and then broke through to the surface. Every Sunday he walked to Belford for the service, eight miles each way, as he didn't approve of the local minister at North Sunderland. But he took sandwiches, so that no one in Belford should be put to the trouble of getting an extra meal on Sundays. He must have looked like something out of the Old Testament, striding through the fields, in storm, rain or sunshine, in his familiar fustian trousers, tail coat and the tall steeple hat that he wore on Sundays.

He had a penetrating, if erratic, sense of humour which, though marred by a little roughness which impeded his perspective at times, always went straight to the root of the problem. He worked all hours of God's daylight and was apt to expect others to do the same, for less reason. He could be very kind — especially to lame dogs such as seamen without a job or widows left with young

Yeavering Bell
— typical of the country in the shadow of the Muckle Cheviot

families. He would invent little, quite unnecessary, jobs for them to do and then pay them more than was usual for doing them. This was to avoid hurting their feelings by offering tactless charity. But curiously enough, it was all kept very quiet especially from his wife and children —partly I think for genuine sensitiveness (in spite of his rough exterior) and partly because he was afraid of being looked upon as a 'bit of a cissy.'

He could be a warm friend but somehow just missed the warmth of common humanity and the wayside virtues that illuminate the blind and the feeble.

His literary tastes were divided between God and current affairs, the daily paper — price 6d in those days— was shared with his old friend Johnnie Railston who had first go at it on alternate weeks. For the rest, he was only ever known to make one exception, in his library, to ecclesiastical works; that was when his sister went out to Canada and, in honour of the occasion, he bought and read 'Uncle Tom's Cabin!'

More seriously though, I don't think he was an egoist because an egoist cannot see beyond the shadow of his own view of life and Alexander would often take advice from those he respected and was even known to sit by while they enlarged upon his spiritual defects — and that is no small form of humility. Like most Northumbrians (for although he was born on the Scottish side he was by now well established on the English side of the border) his theology seems to have been very simple and undogmatic. He accepted without question the fatalism of Calvin and this perhaps explains the unbending severity of his treatment of his children — whom he otherwise loved dearly. One might think that fatalism would lead to apathy but, in Alexander, it seems to have galvanised him to ever harder work and greater expenditure of energy. Having an unspeculative mind, he was less than interested in the thunderings of local priests intent on flattening their spiritual brothers with doctrinal revelations.

I imagine he would have been quite content to follow Martin Luther when he said,

'I do not know it and I do not understand it, but,

sounding from above and ringing in my ears, I hear what is beyond the thought of man'.

His generation of Northumbrians revelled on Sunday in chapel, in the horror of sin, enthusiastically depicted by the Presbyterian divines who intensified its effect upon humanity. But during the week, the soul, cleansed and resurgent, breathed a different air in the grace and freedom of the sea and the countryside. To that age in the first half of the century, Christ was no remote figure or synonym for a general committee ordering the development of the universe; he was a personal figure, based generally on a badly coloured and rather forbidding portrait at the frontispiece of the family Bible. This engendered awe, as it was meant to, as well as personal devotion which could bring out at times not only the stern disciplinarian in Alexander but very human touches and lopsided, but nevertheless genuine and affectionate, moments of real communication.

If he had been a poet instead of a shepherd turned fish curer he might have written at least some celestial rhymes and fairy stories. As it was he had to be content with his celestial music, mostly Psalm settings, Gregorian chants and general church music of which he had a remarkable collection.

To the end he remained a countryman and shepherd rather than a business man. Trout fishing was his only sport except, perhaps, the occasional game of bowls. Old, shiftless or out of work sailors and fishermen from the little harbour of Sea Houses always found a warm corner both in his house and somewhat guarded affections. But above all, I think he got his greatest satisfaction from his trade of fish curer. To him it didn't matter what you did, the important thing was to do it supremely well. It was not good enough just to 'give of your best' that had to be polished by hard work and intelligent application into the ultimate best; whether it was based on fish or figments of the imagination was immaterial.

Like the great army of his work-a-day contemporaries, Alexander left nothing spiritually permanent but I have a pretty shrew notion that when the final sums are done, he and a great host of fellow countrymen will come to be recognised as the strength and permanency of the way of life of that rugged, border land.

CHAPTER III

'IN PREFERENCE TO BLINKY BOBBY'S'

Alexander and Isabella had three sons and three daughters, and of these we shall follow Mary born 1836 and Isabella Catherine (called Kate from now on to avoid confusion) born 1844 and their immediate entourage through the nineteenth century, as guides and pleasant companions. Auntie May was a great character and I shall come back to her, although I was very young when she died. Kate, my grandmother, I remember well and thank goodness she was even then called Kate to avoid worse confusion with her mother.

The children were all brought up strictly but intelligently, as was the custom of the times — with perhaps more of a Scots flavour than English, as was natural. I think from then on, down the next two generations we were all brought up on a diet of Border legend, a great love of the wild things of Cheviot and a healthy respect for the sea.

Sunday was a serious, if not grim, business—salvation or bust. There was a regular attendance at chapel or church for the whole family, though Isabella, their mother, had little in common with her husband's religious beliefs. Much worse, but in tune with the times, the daily family prayers were lengthened and intensified considerably. On Sunday evenings the children read long chapters from the Bible, verse by verse, while old Alexander was always good for the statutory twenty chapters. Except, that is, the night on record when he stopped by mistake at the nineteenth and his wife said with a twinkle in her eye,

'My dear, they have not yet had their complement.'

No wonder poor little James was able to read the

first chapter of St. John's Gospel to a public audience at the age of four.

The North East coast was no place for weaklings in those days of rudimentary medicine. By 1847 Alec (the second son) who was delicate, had been sent first to Alnwick and then to Harrogate for the waters, to get strong; Catherine the eldest daughter was already dead. Being locked in one of the great salt cellars for refusing to eat her porridge may not have helped matters.

For the rest, they went down the road to school, first to Betsy Gold's school and then, because Alexander had his way in matters of educaton, to the Presbyterian School in Back Lane. This was in preference to the rival Church School locally known as 'Blinky Bobby's.'

So each day off they went, wrapped against the cold in their bright tartan plaids which, if the wind was in the South West on the way home, could be unwrapped to do duty as sails.

There was, in the mid-nineteenth century, no shortage of good local schools, each run it seems by a singularly individualistic dominie. To finish their education, both James and Alec were finally sent to Bamburgh, Alec the delicate one, to live with his granny Saunders while James walked the three and a half miles each way, or now and then rode a donkey, which was given the run of the school field during the day. At the age of thirteen he was thought ripe for business, so schooling finished except that, for some years, he had a private tutor to continue his education in Latin and French.

Thus it was that one fateful day, both he and Alec were summoned to the yard and under the supervision of a senior foreman, set to work to construct a small barrel or 'kit'. These the old man examined carefully before giving them the standard test — a good kick. James's barrel held together but poor Alec's fell apart. This settled his future, much to the delight of his mother. As he was obviously going to be no use with his hands,

he would have to work with his head as best he could!
Old Alexander held very firmly that to be good with
your head it was first very necessary to be neat with
your hands and he kept himself in practice all his life.
I have some of his beautiful carving to this day.

As for the girls, it is interesting to recall that at a
time when, apart from finishing schools and other society
institutions for the wealthy, girls in the South certainly
came off very second best when it came to allocation of
the family budget for education, there seems to have been
little or no distinction in the far North. Indeed Mary
was sent to an expensive school in Newcastle when James
was still at Bamburgh. And my grandmother Kate, went
to a well known private school in Edinburgh and shared
what we would now call a flat with brother Alec, while
he finished his degree course. It had been decided, you
remember, after his disastrous attempt at coopering, that
he poor chap, would have to earn his bread and butter
by brain work. He ended up in the ministry.

This incident illustrates, I feel, the apparently contra-
dictory North Countryman's reverence for the academic
training he missed in his own boyhood — and this in
spite of an almost fanatically religious belief in the sanctity
of manual labour and the preachings of Bobby Burns.
Anyway, as an earnest of future endeavours Alec was
deputed to keep the joint accounts during term time in
the flat. If they didn't balance, the difference, I remember
my grandmother saying, was always made up by the
cryptic entry,

'sundries for Kate.'

He was learning fast.

In fact grandmother Kate must have had a 'way' with
her. She seems to have got away with — if not murder—
at least a lot of otherwise jolly irritating little things she
didn't much like or see any point in doing. She hated
embroidery and sewing of any sort and that in an age
when the unfortunate female members of most families

1. Zulus and Skaffies setting out from the Farne Islands 80 years ago

2. Coble and Steam drifter at Tynemouth early 20th century

3. Fishermen in Coble, Budle Bay, end of 19th century

4. Stag Rock Lighthouse — Bamburgh

5. Sea Houses harbour and the Farne Islands

6. Bamburgh Castle from the Village Green

7. Holy Island harbour and castle from the old village

8. The Priory, Lindisfarne

were given very little opportunity to express themselves in creative work in any other way. Fortunately, her elder sister Catherine did beautiful needlework like the bell pull and embroidered dog 'frisk' which are still in the family, together with Aunt Mary's christening robe and cloak made for her nephew's christening and since used by all the Hays and their children from my father downwards. But as Catherine's early death was directly attributed by her father to sitting too long over her sewing, the baby of the family was let off and, I'm afraid, being the ball of fire she was, with a spontaneous sense of humour and very attractive blue eyes, led everybody a whale of a dance. In any case she must have been a breath of air and spring sunshine in that rather dour, Calvinistic household. I gather most of Sea Houses and North Sunderland thought so too and she was much in demand for parties during the holiday time and her father always brought back 'goodies' for her every time he had to go away on business.

It was an odd household, in the middle years of the century. The mother, Isabella Catherine was so busy with the paper work of the family business during the week and with social parties during the weekends (as long as they didn't clash with the Chapel going contingent) that daughter Mary had, between her own schooling and marriage, to do all the housework with one or sometimes two servants to help, and extremely efficiently it was done too by all accounts. Often, sister Kate would be set up on a 'cracket' to dust the cups and saucers on the dresser and the lustre jugs on the higher shelves. I think we are apt in these more casual days to forget the tremendous labour involved in even a small tea party. There would be the 'best china tea service' to be got out of the corner cupboard, with all its attendant silver and linen table clothes and lace mats for the dumb waiters not to mention the great pile of cakes, small and large with delicious 'figure busting' creams and chocolate that the cook and her helpers were busy making in the capacious ovens of the large coal fired range. Then amidst all the bric-a-brac of a mid Victorian drawing room, with its pot plants, ferns and embroidered lace curtains, would sit the grandmother dispensing hospitality and good talk, in her black silk gown, made of such heavy silk it would literally stand up on its own without anyone inside it. No wonder it was handed down to the eldest daughter in due course.

But, the tea parties apart, I find this a quite fascinating period of development especially in this corner of the British Isles. I say British Isles advisedly because the culture, thinking and way of life, of this northern wedge of Northumbria is neither English nor Scots but a unique mixture of both, a sort of Cheviot Borderers' 'free for all' existence. Much of this had come down from the days of cattle thieving and clan warfare to which had been added the seafaring on an inhospitable coast.

This county from Alnwick to Berwick had once been the Anglo Saxon capital of England and before that it had been part of Scotland. At the heart of it was Bamburgh, a miniature Royal city huddled round the gaunt castle on its storm swept bastion of basalt rock formed when Cheviot was a volcano; a hundred feet below the North Sea thundered against the foot of the cliff.

As late as the 19th century, Northumbrians in this corner were bedevilled by much of their Scottish ancestry. They retained the jealous nationalism of the Scots, blended albeit by a practical good sense and opportunism of the Borderer. But there were many who were still prepared to sacrifice peace and fortune to tradition or at least to a peculiar brand of sterile conservatism. Being well to the North of the mining and industrial belt round Newcastle and Durham in the South, they had escaped the worst excesses of poverty and slum housing. They were individualists from necessity, forcing a living from bleak moorlands and a hungry sea and you find little trace of the class barriers of the South; a man whatever his status or calling was still a man 'for a' that.' The farm labourer sat down with the yeoman farmer at his board and the squire or laird was generally a slightly more prosperous farmer, many of whom were indeed busy becoming gentlemen. The landlords, if not philanthropists, at least didn't exploit their lands primarily for profit.

The resurgence of Presbyterian or Calvinistic religious observance of which Alexander is a good example, was typical of the reaction not only to 18th century licence and morals as typified by the later Restoration Dramatists but to the Jacobin influence on the continent. As a result, Sunday observance was revived (one is apt to forget how recent this is) and lasted well into the next century, added to which at least two of my female cousins apparently carried away by this wave of religious fervour became missionaries in darkest China for reasons best known to themselves. I have ample reason to remember, because they used to write twenty-two page 'newsy letters' and we had to sit after breakfast while these hideous documents were read out to two fidgety small boys.

On the other hand by this time the isolation of these remote parts of England was gradually being broken down by the coming of the railways which were causing the whole world to huddle together in thought and in the acceptance of a more universal code of behaviour. In 1847 even Sea Houses had been brought near the rest of England by the main line of the North Eastern Railway which went through Chathill only five miles away. Later, a single tracked branch line was to run down to North Sunderland and Sea Houses itself.

Mutual Improvement Societies, another sign of the times, were springing up everywhere. They discussed, according to my records, quite an enchanting range of subjects, including,

'Happiness and where is it to be found?'
'Is there such a thing as chance?'
'Is there more matter now than at the Creation?'

In the course of which last subject I can only assume that accurate evidence must have been hard to come by!

Kate's two brothers Alec and James were enthusiastic members, even to the well remembered occasion when, on the subject of 'Do animals think?', James's friend Willie Milliken who had been cogitating for half an hour got slowly to his feet and said solemnly,

"Yes, I do think that they do think,'
and sat down agan to recover from the effects of this profundity.

But I don't want to give the impression that the records are all of sermon and Mutual Improvement Societies, not a bit of it. Even on Sundays when secular reading was barred there was Pilgrim's Progress, with all the excitement of journeys over moorland and hill in not at all unfamiliar scenery, and the beautiful lucidity of the prose, which I suppose has never been equalled except in King James's version of the Bible, must have done as much to lay a foundation of literary appreciation for the youngsters as it did for me in the years to come. During the week days and especially those free from necessity to go to school, there was never a dull moment — on the moors guddling trout, helping the hill shepherds or just playing Scots and English in mock raids. It was a wonderful carefree world, full of wizards and knights and princesses in every fold of the hills. The moss trooping and raiding had to be done, at best, on borrowed ponies and the old donkey commandeered surreptitiously from a friendly aunt or, more often than not, on foot.

The best fun of all was, of course, when they were judged to be experienced enough to take the family coble out and fish or pit their sailing skill against the other boys whose parents owned boats which were not always in use. The 'Raiding' went on but this time in a much more exciting medium. The attacking force were generally Danes and the defenders Saxons or Britons as the mood took them.

Long before they were allowed out of the harbour alone, however, the popular ploy was to get Alexander or one of the Darlings who sailed across to buy provisions from the mainland, to take them over to the Farnes for a picnic and a ramble round the cliffs, collecting birds' eggs or fishing in the Kettle. Alexander liked taking a day off to sail over to William Darling for a 'bit crack' about music or wildlife or other of their mutual interests. Sometimes the children wanted the run and he found an excuse to fetch a barrel or two of herring that William's sons had caught. Then, while old men yarned in the cosy kitchen with Georgiana brewing up strong tea, the boys would be off with the Darling sons to explore the nearby islands or whatever the parents had decreed the weather suitable for.

Best of all were the summer days when the boys were invited to stay the night on the Longstone and on the following day would accompany the younger William Darling (now officially appointed assistant Lighthouse keeper) on his rounds to the more distant Farnes. If William picked them up in Sea Houses, when his weekly provisioning was done, they would sail to the Inner Farne where the first lighthouse, a square tower with a coal fire on top, was built. The outer one was on Staple Island until 1826 when it was moved to the Brownsman. Oil replaced coal about 1809. The South side, as I well remember on my own trips later, was an awesome rampart of basalt cliffs, home only to sea birds. To the North was the Churn, a natural fissure in the rocks, so formed as to squirt a jet of water high into the air with an onshore wind. Apart from Prior Castell's Tower and the ruins of the fish house there is, of course, the hallowed ground of St Cuthbert's Chapel, which was about this time (1848) in process of being restored by Archbishop Thorpe.

There are no remains prior to the 14th century with the possible exception of the well which is in Prior Castell's Peel tower now. But for all that, this is the most mystical and sacred piece of ground in Northumbria. After St Aidan came St Cuthbert to stay for nine years as a hermit and resigning his bishopric in 676, to stay in a small circular cell and keep sheep and grow his own crops on this windswept island. People flocked from all over the known world to receive his blessing and drink of the wells where no fresh water was before. As far as I remember it was appallingly brackish and more like

St. Cuthbert's Chapel and Prior Castell's Pele Tower
on the Inner Farne — as they were last century

the stuff we used to find on a disused desert oasis when I was serving in Arabia, but I expect they had stronger stomachs in Saxon times. Then, as now, the rocks would be strewn with sea campion and the landing was always at the little stage in St Cuthbert's Cove, in what we called the Kettle — the only reasonably sheltered anchorage in less than five fathoms.

To the East lay the Wideopens (Wedums as they were called) and the little Scarcar and Big Scarcar which were generally covered with foam. To the West lay the Swedman (covered at high water like the Glororum Shad) and the Elbow and the South Goldstone, and the Megstone which had collected more wrecks than any other of the 28 Islands.

Across the Fairways, the boys generally landed at Staple and then the Brownsman — more basalt cliffs and screaming birds. They support practically no vegetation and the birds' eggs are more difficult to get at, because many of the pinnacles of rocks are separated from the main cliffs by twelve foot gulleys, each 200 feet deep. At that time there was a bird keeper on the Brownsman who supervised the collection of eggs by the boys who were allowed so many each.

The keeper lived in a cottage during the summer, much I suppose as St Cuthbert used to do except that he had the lighthouse keeper's family on the Longstone for company now and then, in fact he grew cabbages and potatoes for them. The Wamses were generally the next call, the landing would be made on North Wamses among the nests of eider duck beloved of the old monks because they were less noisy than their neighbours, the cormorants. The stink used to be appalling!

From there, beyond Big and Little Harcar, Piper Gut and the Midden Gut with its six knot tide at High Water Springs lies the Longstone where the Darling family lived in the lighthouse. The only Farnes more remote still were the Knavestones, beyond the Hares to the North and the bare Crumstone to the south, south-east. There was a fairly sheltered landing place where parties of visitors sometimes landed in fine weather and here the boys would pull up the boat on the rollers out of the reach of the tide. Walter White went there in 1858 and says,

'Grace Darling's sister, a quiet middle aged looking woman of respectful manner, welcomed us to the light house and led the way up to the sitting room. It has a comfortable look, and something more with its collection of books, natural curiosities, engravings of the memorable rescue and family portraits. Doubly precious must have been a library in such a spot! . . . After a little talk we went up to the lantern and out upon the gallery, whence, the tower being sixty three feet high, there is a good prospect over the islands . . . Here, nearly six miles from the shore, the isolation appears something awful!'
And this was a nice fine day. He does add,
'The Longstone, rising but four feet above high water mark is swept by every gale with fierce drifts of spray and foam.'
Indeed during a bad gale the Darlings were often forced to seek refuge in the upper stories of the lighthouse and the chickens and the domestic animals were locked in a sort of block house below. However, the prospect of a gale only added to the excitement of the youngsters as they fished and cleaned and gutted their catch or hunted for crabs and lobsters. They were simple pleasures in those days and none the less intense or satisfying for that. In any case it was freedom from school, though not entirely from 'chalk and chapel' because old Father Darling was about as tough a Presbyterian as Alexander Ewing and regarded all card games as the work of the devil. 'Chalk' was the universal cure (by the tablespoonful) for all tummy troubles!

Anyway, back on the mainland, the world was changing slowly but inexorably.

As a sign of which, trades unions had been made legal in 1825 when Joseph Hume persuaded the Commons to repeal Pitt's Combination Act; though it still didn't affect Alexander's Fish Curing Yard staff and workers who were perfectly happy to trust to his sense of fair play and general humanity. Just over the Cheviots, wool mills were rising in Hawick and Jedburgh, and even Melrose. Further off, cotton was creating the need for slums and industrial sprawl in villages such as Lanark, Renfrew and Ayr with social results so well set out in Galt's *Annals of the Parish*. Published in 1821, I still think this is one of the most revealing and human documents ever written about Scotland in this painful period of change.

But let us return to our womenfolk because I think that they were, as ever, the best barometer of changing times. Skirts were getting shorter and even walking was beginning to be regarded as a possible pastime, to be indulged in in moderation only of course, and suitably chaperoned. Finally, the bicycle put an end to all pretence of regulated propriety and completed the emancipation. Middle class young ladies read Byron and Scott while some, like Jane Austen, Maria Edgworth and Hannah More even had the leisure to write their own books.

Along the Beadnell, Bamburgh, Holy Island and Berwick strip of coast, it was in fact the little family businesses like Alexander's Fish Curing Yards which, in default of larger concerns, gave the women of North Sunderland, Sea Houses and Beadnell their first taste of real and complete independence. The money they earned while their menfolk were away at sea was their own and they kept it. No longer was it necessary to scrape up hard earned pin money by keeping backyard chickens, mending nets or doing domestic work for their wealthier sisters. As bargainers they were tough and would stand no flannel or nonsense but, when they worked, the fish guts fairly flew across the bench.

Life could still be very hard for women of, what I suppose the modern sociologists would call the middle classes, though as I have explained the edges of class were very blurred in 19th century Northumberland. There were no women's universities or colleges at Oxford or Cambridge and very few professional outlets even for the trained woman if the early death of her husband left her unprovided for. I remember my grandmother telling me of her Aunt Mary who had married the captain (Gibbons) of a coastal trading brig which brought in sufficient for their needs until like so many more, it was wrecked off the Farnes one wild night with loss of all lives including

The Herring Yard
(from a contemporary engraving)

her husband's. I don't think she ever really gave up hope that, by some miracle, he might return some day and she would spend hours of her precious spare time gazing across at the Farnes from the harbour wall.

Unfortunately this Mrs Gibbons was a shy, retiring and rather sweet person, with no private income or professional training except a taste for literature and serious music. However, much to everyone's surprise, and with probably a flash of typical North country toughness, she departed to relatives near Perth and opened a small shop which did well enough to keep her and her baby son in reasonable comfort. But fate hadn't finished with her yet. A stove by the cot flared up one evening while she was

serving customers in the shop and the blankets caught
fire and the baby was fatally burnt.

Back she came to Sea Houses and started all over
again, with another little shop in what is still called 'The
Nick'. This was an alleyway one used to pass through
by the Hay's Herring Yard. She worked up a good trade
in spite of being too kind hearted to compel payment
for goods from fisher folk in times when catches were
bad. Unfortunately the few ne'er-do-wells traded on this.
I take off my hat to her. Still she never gave up hope
and after work would go alone to the cliff by the harbour
and sit straining her dark handsome eyes into the gathering dusk away over the distant islands. What a contrast
she was, to her sister who was a kind of professional
sufferer! When her engagement to the local parson was
broken off she seems to have spent the rest of her melancholy, selfish life, impressing her nephews and nieces with
the beauty and saintliness of her character.

It is difficult to leave the middle years of the century
without a brief word about one or two of the many
delightful Northumbrian characters who feature in the
family records. I think it is the two local Presbyterian
ministers that come most readily to mind, each in his
own way typical of their age — Mr Glover of the Old
Kirk and Donald Munroe of the Back Lane. The former
was very tall, courtly and spoke in broad lowland Scots.
His only little difficulty in kirk was, apparently, certain
lapses of memory; among those best remembered being,
an occasion when he was dealing with Zaccheus in his
sermon and had to turn in the pulpit and call to a friend,

'Ay! John, what did they ca' the wee mannie that
climbed up into the tree?'

or he would finish,

'In the words of that well known hymn—
Aye, but I find I've forgotten them.'

He was a kindly man and even his shaky memory
could be made to function if he came across anyone in

need. One day, it is recorded, he gave a lift in his gig to an old woman who was walking to what she called 'the occasion,' meaning the Lord's supper and told Mr Glover she was looking forward to hearing him preach.

'Where are you sleeping?', he asked. To which she replied confidently,

'The Lord will dootless provide.'

The reverend gentleman expressed some doubts as to the Lord's reliability in this matter. During the service, however, at the end of the sermon and before the blessing he looked round the church and said,

'Where's the auld wife I gave a lift to?'

'Here I am, sir,' came a shrill voice from the back.

'Aweel I have a bed for ye. Ye're to sleep wi' Dickie Henderson's lass. An' now to God the Father, God the Son, etc.'

He once mounted into the pulpit and felt in his tail-coat pocket. After a pause he leant over the rail and said to his faithful housekeeper,

'Annie I fear we've committed a mistake, the day. You maun just gang hame and get my sermon out of ma breek's pocket while I bide a wee.'

And, best of all, I remember and treasure,

'I shall not be with you next Lord's Day — for reasons best known to myself.'

What all this rather cosy talk illustrates, I think, is that preachers, especially in the border lands, whether Church or Non-Conformist, had a much more personal and free and easy relationship with their congregations, both in and out of kirk than exists today.

With the wrong temperament it could, of course, develop almost into a feud, as when a well known fire eater finished a tirade against the sin of drunkenness with,

'We'll no mak this discoorse owre personal; but if a short, bald-headed laird sitting in the corner of the East gallery pew tak's it to himsel', I canna help it.'

I myself, have heard, halfway through the twentieth century — a hundred years later — a remote country parson in the Irish Free State whose red faced, hard riding manner might have stepped straight out of Addison's *Spectator,* lambast a whole congregaton in true eighteenth century style. As near as I can remember it went,

'And now ye miserable, crawling sinners. D'ye hear the rain? — Aye. D'ye hear the dunder of the thunder? — Aye. And y're thinking about your ruined crops — aye and who d'ye blame — the Lord! — as usual.

'And you know pairfectly well in your innards, ye worms, it's your ain fault. Two weeks ago you were given the signs by the good Lord; the windy sky the signs of weather breaking that could be read by any unconscious cow — an' did ye heed them? No. Ye were far too busy drinking and mak'in quick money with the early tatie crop. An' now ye're too late — and you blame the Lord.'

Here he slowly and dramatically surveyed the whole congregation and then added sorrowfully,

'Ye miserable — crawlin' — sinners.'

And so it went on for three quarters of an hour and they loved it. They wriggled and cringed and exchanged satisfied glances; the church was full. At the end of this extraordinary oration, I remember, we solemnly got up and sang 'God save the King.' Good for the Irish Free State!

But to return to the mid nineteenth century. Certain words came to stand for the complete thought. For instance, Alexander would say, meaning breakfast or dinner,

'Will ye take your haddock wi' us the day?'

And I think he would have appreciated the cautious countryman who, when asked if he could play the Northumbrian bagpipes replied,

'I couldna say for certain; foreby, I havena ever tried.'

One thing no one will deny, it is a truly spartan climate, especially when the November fogs close in. I can remember my father telling me the famous story of how Miss Hetty missed her own funeral, through being left out on top of a dyke. Miss Hetty, you must know, was a formidable lady, known far and wide as the housekeeper of a retired sea captain called Robert Logan. I don't think I ever knew Mis Hetty's other name but one day, the story goes, she sent for her nephew and said,

> 'Andy I'm deein' and as you'll have charge o' my bits and pieces, mind you see the folks a' git the same amount of whisky at the funeral as they did at my baptism — no more, no less.'

Andy said 'aye' but forgot to ask what the baptismal amount was and on the day, thought it best to let each have what he seemed to need. His Aunt Hetty, he reflected philosophically, had always been a kindly understanding soul.

Well, it was November and the afternoons closing in and ten miles to walk from the captain's house to the kirk. Fortunately there was an inn half way, where, under the captain's directions they rested. It was finally decided, that as the pub floor didn't seem quite the right place for Aunt Hetty, she would be happier outside — on top of a moorland dyke from which, anyway, she would be more accessible afterwards.

Eventually, when they got to the churchyard it was well and truly dark and the gravedigger, who had been waiting all afternoon, was in a rare taking, not to mention the minister. In fact neither were in any mood to accept the good captain's explanation of why the cortege was so far behind schedule. By that time the sexton was seen looking anxiously round —

'Whaur's Miss Hetty?'

'In her coffin, to be sure,' said the Captain and added,

'An' we'd best get her in the ground as soon as maybe.'

The trouble was — there was no coffin! Miss Hetty was, the Captain and mourners slowly realised, still atop the dyke five miles back, outside the inn — or so they hoped!

The interment had to be put off officially till the next day and an anxious little party of those in the least bad shape set off, I gather, to retrieve Miss Hetty before it was too late.

The other Sea Houses' minister, Donald Munroe, was a very different character. He was large, dark and had an enormous voice and sense of his own importance as well as a great way with the whisky decanter. The villagers for long remember his prayer during a wet harvest,

'Oh Lord send us some wind to dry the folk's corn, not a ranting, tanting, tearing wind but just a huthering duthering wind to dry the folk's corn.'

On one occasion he had a South Country guest minister to assist him and stiffened him with the promise of a good glass of hot whisky toddy after service — 'and no washy duty paid whisky at that,' he added. When his colleague murmured something about smuggling being contrary to the Act of Parliament, the Reverend Donald snorted and said,

'Acts of Parliament are apt to lose their breath before they reach Sea Houses.'

Once, when he exhorted his congregation to practise honesty, as being the best policy, he added in a reflective aside from the pulpit,

'I hae tried baith.'

And as my grandmother used to say,

'He ribbled off the prayers as if he were leading a cavalry charge.' Nor, indeed, was there much encouragement to folk about to get wed. The ceremony was apt to be prepared by a fierce look from under the shaggy eyebrows and then,

'My friends, marriage is a blessing to a few, a curse to many and a great unsairtainty to us all.'

But there was at least one occasion when he seems to have come off second best. A neighbouring Roman Catholic priest with whom he was on surprisingly friendly terms often visited Sea Houses in a gig pulled by an ancient pony. One day he appeared behind a new animal and was greeted by the Presbyterian priest with,

'What's come o' the old faithful?'

'He's died minister.'

'Ah weel, nay doot ye gave him the full offices of the church!'

To which his R.C. friend replied sweetly,

'Na. I didna dae that. You see, he turned Seceder before he died — so I just buried him like a beast.'

The kindest note on which to take our leave of Donald Munroe, for better or worse, is a homely and so typical conversation of some old women, going home from the Back Lane Chapel. One was heard to say,

'My, the auld diel was in gran' form the nicht. Special like, when he says, "Raphael sings, an Gabriel strikes his goolden harp an' a' the angels clap their wings wi' joy . . ." My . . . but it waur gran', it got me thinkin' o' our ain geese in t'back yeard when they turn to the South an' clap their wings 'cos they smell rain coming after a bad drooth.'

It would surely be difficult to get nearer to God than that sincerely meant simple praise straight from the good earth.

To return to the family, the Scottish side of the border seems to have gone on providing most of the husbands and wives of Alexander's family. Apart from his daughter Kate's husband, my grandfather Thomas Hay who came from Hawick, his sister Isabella married one

of the Haigs of Duns and Bemersyde, a bit to the North
West of Hawick.

'Betide, betide, whate'er betide,

There shall aye be a Haig in Bemersyde."
runs the old prophecy of Thomas of Ercildoune. The
family have, indeed been there since the days of Malcolm
the Maiden and the tower is next to Swailholme where
Scott spent much of his youth. As Andrew Lang says,

The Eildon Hills across the Tweed by Bermersyde

"There was scarce a border battle in which the Haigs
did not leave a representative on the field.'

The only two other things I remember about the Haigs
both concern fishing. Apparently one of the family had
beaten up some of the brethren of the Abbey of Melrose
and his heirs were condemned to pay a dozen salmon
yearly until they became so scarce that the fine was com-

muted to money because no fish could be caught. The other yarn concerned a 70 pound fish whose head was alleged to have been too large to get into the landing net!

Anyway, Thomas Haig of Duns must have caught a tartar in my great aunt who was noted for her temper and an even more austere and melancholy outlook than her brother Alexander. He seems to have marched her smartly off (complete with four sons and a daughter) to Canada in 1835 where, I am told, their descendants multiply mightily.

Old Alexander duly died in 1869 and three years later his son James married and brought his wife to live in the old home, while Alec and his mother built a new house (now called Mayfield) out of some old cottages called Molly's because old Molly Carr used to live in one of them. And so, with the marriage of daughter Kate to my grandfather Thomas Hay of Hawick in 1872, a new generation of Hays and Ewings were loosed upon the Northumberland countryside.

As we take leave of him, I can't help admitting to a bit of a soft spot for old Alexander. He may have been a bit set in his Calvinistic ways in his later years but he never lost his sense of humour, odd though it may have been, or his humanity, and his reputation for just dealing with his work folk. Above all, he retained his soft spot for lame dogs.

During his 84 years he had been successively, shepherd, cooper, merchant seaman, master of some coastal brigs and originator and owner of a successful firm of Fish Curers providing much needed employment for those not actually manning the boats in the two fishing villages of Sea Houses and North Sunderland. So successful was the business that Jean Terry of St Andrews writing as lately as 1913 could still start a description of this part of the coast,

‘At Sea Houses is an extensive fish curing establishment.’

But I have a sneaking feeling that, successful though this practical and unromantic venture was, he always recalled with most affection the one imaginative venture that failed —the running of a small line of coastal craft to rush delicious Northumbrian delicacies down the storm bound coast and up the Thames to London. It failed but it must have been fun while it lasted.

And as for the lame dogs, well, as Corporal Trim would have said,

'For that, he shall go to heaven.'

CHAPTER IV

'SHE'S HAME BUT SHE'S NO IN'

For the flavour of the border country during the remainder of the century and up to the first world war where I can take over from personal memory ,I will continue to use the results of long talks with my grandmother when she recalled local events, the notes written down by her daughters and cousins and numerous letters that have survived family spring cleans. Apart from her eldest son, my father Thomas Hay (again I'm afraid with the same Christian name as her husband) Kate had four sons and two daughters to whom she seems to have been single mindedly devoted. Like many another in those parts she rebelled against her strict Presbyterian upbringing and became instead a church woman. She was always a delightful companion with, I am glad to say, a delicious sense of humour that lasted until her death in 1917. It was something that just bubbled up and danced all over anybody that happened to be around — even when her coloured parasol, was tweaked out of her hand by an envious puff of wind and blown away to sea.

It was the era of great family picnics which, somehow, the menfolk not actually at sea or away on business, managed to find time to join in. Out came the old phaeton and away they would go to Budle Bay with its razor shells that I remember so well, or to Embleton, where in summer the wide sweep of grassy common was a riot of wild geranium with its rich reddish purple blossoms and banks of thyme and marjoram sparkled between the gorse bushes. I get a very strong impression that grandmother Kate and her sister-in-law Annie King didn't let much grass grow under their feet and from what I remember of them in their old age I can well imagine the speed at which

Sea Houses was kept turning over in their younger days.

For some years, they went together for French conversation to an old sweetie called Ralph Morton and I don't think he really knew quite what had hit him. The two would come home wagging their fingers at each other and repeating,

"You perceive my love that . . . .'

but it was all kindly meant and I think he really enjoyed the ragging as much as they did.

Just as warm hearted but much more serious, were Kate's deep and lifelong relationships with some of her old boyfriends and childhood loves, especially the Morris boys of what is now called Scot's Farm. I can remember the look in her eyes as she spoke of one in particular when both were in ripe old age, and as a boy I often thought what fun it would have been to have them meet once again and then to have settled them down into their chairs with a drink and closed the door quietly upon them.

Scot's Farm was haunted and many's the tale circulating in Sea Houses about the noises and their origins. I get the impression that not a few were indeed circulated by the Morris's coachman who, in the hospitable confines of the Bambro' Inn, was noted for his skill at exchanging pints of Ram Tam from strangers for a wide range of ingenious 'true stories.'

Some must have been authentic and in any case no one living in the 1860's or 70's along the coast from Sea Houses to Holy Island would have entertained a moment's doubt as to their truth. He had a staunch corroborator in the maid in the Harbour House opposite. They used to 'compare notes' when he rubbed down the horses late at night after a social visit to another family or a late dance.

You see, they were actually living in, what was in those days, one of the most notorious houses, not only in Sea Houses but in the whole of the Border country. Maria Marten and her murder in the Red Barn had nothing on the notorious Dr Bellany of real life drama in the local papers of those Victorian days. I remember being told about him in hushed tones and indeed the family records do him full justice.

In the Morris House there had lived, ten or fifteen years earlier in the century, a widow, of trusting and agreeable temperament called Mrs Skelly, and, as you will have guessed, and I quote,

'her gentle beautiful daughter.'

Well, apparently all the young bloods in Sea Houses and Bamburgh had fallen for her in a big way; even my uncle James was a bit breathless, as were a great many other suitors from the county between the sea and Cheviot. With the name of Rose she was of course called 'The Rose of the North.' I gather she had not only a powerful aura of 'come hither' but was fairly catholic in her tastes and grandma's brother wasn't the only one who had been promised 'she would wait for him.' Time passed happily with all the worker bees buzzing eagerly round the honey pot.

Then, one summer day, the blow fell. Perhaps I should explain that during the spring a strange, and to the locals most suspicious, character had come to the village. He went by the name of Dr Bellany. Nobody could find out where he came from or what his qualifications were. But he had a little house built near the quarry on the South side of Sea Houses harbour, half in a cave which incidentally still goes by the name of 'Bellany's Cave.' It was an extraordinary edifice, built very low and with its chimney only just level in height with the top of the bank.

This was gossip enough for a May morning along the quay but many a young heart missed more than a beat when it became known a day or so later, that the 'Rose of the North' had fallen so completely and unexpectedly for his charms that they had been married on the quiet. To the astonished gaze of the village, Bellany calmly took over Mrs Skelly's house and turned the key for good on the cave dwelling. He then planned how to get rid of the old lady. This wasn't difficult as she was rather frail and a drive together which ended in a convenient upset soon finished her off. Rose herself was next on his list but, from the evidence which came out at the subsequent trial, she proved a much tougher proposition and he had to prepare the ground a little.

Eventually she was persuaded to go to London with him for a holiday and to do some shopping. Poison was the method chosen for her departure and it come out in the trial evidence that there had been two glasses by the bedside with the poisoned drink placed nearer Rose. She seems to have mopped it up and faded for good.

The trial itself, which was a cause celèbre, dragged on for weeks but in the end, the jury couldn't agree and so Bellany was, to everyone's astonishment, released. The man must have had the most colossal gall, because back he comes to the village (Sea Houses) as bold as brass with some of his friends, in spite of all the newspaper publicity. This was too much for the local fishermen. Led by Rob Wilson, a student parson, they attacked him in his house. He defended himself with a revolver and was only driven into the open when the house was burnt down about his head. He escaped to France where he remained until his death long after the turn of the century.

His escape didn't end the festivities at Sea Houses. Five fishermen had supported Bellany and consequently their life-like effigies were burnt in a wild sort of Viking ceremony one black night at the end of the long pier, with the shafts of firelight snaking across the inky water of the harbour — the fifies, skaffies and other boats having been carefully removed at high water and moored farther down the quay out of harm's way. The effigy of the doctor himself was lashed to the chimney of the Harbour House, from whence the flames could be seen from as far away as North Sunderland and Bamburgh. Ah well, no wonder the old house was a bit haunted by its memories by the time the Morrison family bought it and moved in.

There were many other famous village characters of the time, including old Railston the professional miser and his daughter who was,

'fair and tall and had a good figure, not pretty, but with such charm of manner that one quite forgot her lack of actual beauty.'

She came adrift eventually over Dr MacDonald a very eligible young man who was practising at that time in the 'toon' and used to flash by in his fashionable basket phaeton but I'm afraid neither of them add much to our knowledge of life towards the end of the century.

Far more important to the scene was a grand race of people that have since disappeared from the modern world and would in any case have had few actual counterparts in the South. I mean the North Country and Scots Border family servants, who would have held their own in any society and without whom no account of the period would be complete. Anything less 'servile' than these cornerstones of the establishment would be hard to imagine. Mostly they ruled the roost with a rod of iron, kept the place and policies as they should be kept and had the children well under their thumb, the last being done by a skilful combination of stern theoretical facade and warm kindly practice — especially on baking days and when pre-party goodies were to be found in greater than usual profusion about the kitchen. I was frankly terrified of them, and so I think, were most other small boys. I know we had had a certain amount of practice with our nannies but it wasn't the same thing. Your nannie was more or less accessible and you got used to her little ways and soon devised various means of exploiting her weaknesses to your own advantage, which is probably the nearest you could hope, at that early age, to come to getting your own way.

The North country family servant had no weaknesses

to exploit, as far as I was ever able to discover. Anyway, the process of finding out would almost savour of setting out to fix God. But for all that they were a grand lovable lot. Sweeties like Jenny Redford in the 1870's whose tactful,

'She's hame but she's no in,'

when her mistress didn't want company, have become part of North Country legend. Everybody must have known the Morton's Scotch Jean, who was renowned at hogmanay parties and border ceilidhs for her impersonations of Alexander the Great, complete with black moustache, broadsword and plaid of some totally unknown and supposedly Greek clan. The children loved it and looked forward to the annual performance with the greatest glee.

On Sunday there was singing, not unnaturally, in the little English church (Episcopalian) and so the clergyman was quickly dubbed thhe 'Whistle-Kirk minister.' Jean, who was by way of being a very strict Presbyterian, was taken there one day for a change, in the family carriage, and was heard to say afterwards in a reflective moment,

'Oh aye, it was verra bonny, verra bonny, but oh my, it's an awfu' way of spending the Sabbath.'

I think, also, she could never understand why the minister 'wore his sark (shirt) above his coat' while the proper ones wore it underneath, like other decent folk.

But even chapel had to take its proper place in the general order of things, as when her mistress came panting up the stairs calling out,

'Look there, look there — what is it?' and added,
'Oh God, the chapel's on fire.'

Jean's only reply was,

'Is that a' ma'am — what a fright ye gave me. I thought for aye minute the parlour fire had gone out.'

Northumbrians are not given to flowery eulogies of each other or mutual friends, let alone household staff. The furthest they let themselves go as a general rule is,

E

'Aweel, she's a very decent old body.'
but there was the day one mistress was speaking thus
of a possible cook for a forthright old lady and was told,
'Damn her decency — can she make good collops!'

On reflection, the most characteristic trait of border
folk is the very natural down to earth acceptance of life
and death and the inevitableness of the natural cycle of
things even after death. The church, chapel or whatever
religious institution, was not only respected as being an
outpost of the next world but as the homely, natural
and visible form of the higher direction of the present
world of sun and wind and rain. If a husband's winding
sheet were too long, it wasn't wasted. A strip might be
cut off to make a couple of spare mutch caps for his
widow without any disrespect for the owner. I remember
being told of a conversation which I think puts the feeling
in a nutshell. The folk were from Bamburgh but had long
been living in Newcastle and the wife was dying. It went
roughly thus,

'Well John, we're going to part — have I been a
gude wife?'

'Aye just middlin' Jenny, just middlin',' says John,
not I may say, implying the least criticism of a wife to
whom he was utterly devoted. But simply from habit of
a lifetime, being unwilling to commit himself without
proper consideration.

'John,' she continues, 'Ye maun promise me to bury
me in Bambro' in the auld kirkyard beside mither
an' the family. I wad never feel at peace among unco
strange folk in the dirt and smoke o' Newcastle.'

John thinks a bit and then says soothingly,

"Weel, weel, Jenny my ain woman, we'll just try you
in a nice bit shady corner of St John's here first
and sine, if you dinna lie quiet, we'll just pit ye back
in Bambro.'

It is a wonderful dry, matter of fact borderer's view
of the most serious subject, which comes quite inevitably

to all of us and there is something richer in its dark simplicity than many a more flowery reaction of the Southerner.

I suppose Bessie Scott (Mrs Durham) who was maid and friend of my Auntie May (Mrs William King) for years and whose loving care embraced both her and her house at Mayfield, is the personality that comes to mind most readily when one looks back to these times. Not only does she keep popping up with delightful frequency in the notes, but so often did she and Auntie May find their way into the conversation of my elders when I was very young that I find it difficult to believe they would no longer appear, welcoming and beaming happiness, in the porch of the old house if I took it into my head to walk across the fields from Sea Houses and open the wicket gate at the bottom of the garden.

The flavour of life in the two villages comes as much from long talks with Bessie in later life as from Mrs King's long newsy letters to my mother which I still have, and my grandmother's own reminiscences. And what better way to fill in the years from 1880 to 1910 by staying in this so typically Northumbrian home. As I said earlier, family maids tended to become indistinguishable from other old friends and Bessie recalls, not only the strict standards of cleanliness and straight dealing of the Aunt with anyone who called but, with warm affection, she used to talk of the comfortable evenings spent together, either in Butt or Ben, it didn't matter which. It depended only which had the most cheerful fire. There she would listen for hours, sometimes with neighbours who had dropped in, sometimes alone, to Mary King taking off, in a kindly but devastating way, all the pompous characters in the neighbourhood.

At Christmas times there was a great family gathering including many whose work had taken them South and who came North for Christmas and the traditional Hogmanay. This was done somehow, and hordes of hungry children fed, in spite of the Aunt's rather straightened circumstances after the death of her husband and spasmodic ill health. But even more important to the village was the care for the sick and the out of work. Bessie was constantly helping to prepare hot soups and at other times custards and small buckets of goodies to be taken to those in need. Sometimes the postman took them on his rounds and sometimes a passing neighbour would drop in and ask if there were any 'messages' (parcels) or to give news of someone having got well or another candidate for a wee strengthening bite.

Their own Sunday dinner was always very simple so that mistress and maid could each attend their separate churches. Beefsteak pudding and a good milk pudding seem to have been the usual fare.

The callers were far too numerous to set down but all seemed to be welcome. Bessie recalls especially Mr Clark the Coastal Missionary who always used to call at the North door (Bessie's end of the house) on his arrival at Sea Houses of a Saturday night, 'just to make sure of his dinner on Sunday.' At which time, according to my grandmother, he would solemnly thank 'bountiful Jehovah' for each separate dish as it was brought in by Bessie.

I cannot help taking my hat right off to the Aunt over many of these characters that she cheerfully coped with month after month. Being herself of a very shrewd and quick wit and a wonderful raconteur in both English and Lowland Scots it must have been most trying for her to have to listen to dreary gossip, and not being able to turn it off without hurting the feelings of the older ministers and neighbours, which she would be much too kind hearted to contemplate.

Like sister Kate, she had certain little affairs which, because of the censorious times, were kept very strictly under control but I gather she had that sort of twinkle in the eye and managed to retain her looks well into later life. The real tragedy of her life had been a young Roman Catholic, with whom she fell in love long before William King came into the picture. But you can just imagine the reception he must have got from her mother and Calvinistic father. In those days you just couldn't tell them all gently to go and take a long run and jump into North Sea.

However, like everything else, she faced up to it without visible diminution of outward sparkle which must have taken some doing. Then she married the next best thing, became an early widow and, resilient as ever, more or less took the whole village into her sweep of kindly awareness. How she tolerated children roaring round her meticulously spotless house with its irreplaceable family china and books and silver Lares and Penates, the village never knew — nor did the family.

There were of course limits; my father, baby Tom at that stage, was sternly forbidden to play 'waterfalls' down the front stairs with buckets of pebbles from the drive. And another nephew, unfamiliar with her direct ways and speech got a bit of a bounce off when he proudly presented his fiancèe to, as he thought, a doting aunt and got a smile and with a little resigned sigh — 'poor fellow.'

She was a great traveller in whatever spare time she could manage and while Bessie would continue to run Mayfield, the Aunt would take any member of the family not otherwise getting a proper holiday, with her. Much of her time in Sea Houses was spent helping her brother James and his son John Ewing who, for over forty years, superintended the non sectarian Sunday School of Sea Houses, held in the 'Peige.' James had taken over the family business from his father Alexander in 1869 and was now equally well known and liked. James, incidentally, was a staunch Liberal and Sir Edward (later Viscount) Grey of Falloden recalls with much gratitude that it was James, as Chairman of the Berwick-on-Tweed Division of

Northumberland first proposed him as a candidate for Parliament in 1885.

Then, in 1910, both of them died and grandmother Kate followed in 1917. I can't help thinking that Sea Houses and the little villages round about were poorer for their passing. I think they were the last of the border clan of Ewings and Hays that had both their feet planted in Northumbrian tradition, whether battling for a living from the land or from the sea. They 'belonged' and of their being and the thousands like them, is the stuff of this Border Country. A little dour perhaps at times in their humour but then the Border Country can itself be a bit dour. They, like their ancestors, worked, fought and played hard and, above all, what they did — and they earned their livings at an odd assortment of trades and professions — they gave of their best and that best turned out to be pretty good. Furthermore, when life had given them so much, they returned the compliment and each before his death could feel that they had at least tried to put back, through service on public committees or by teaching in Sunday schools, a bit of a return contribution to the 'kitty' of life as a 'thank you' for having had the good fortune to be born into one of the most delectable countries the British Isles has to offer as a birth place.

Sadly, I have to say that there will be no more like them. We have all drifted away from the Border country to make our livings in impersonal professions. My father started the rot. After he and his brother William had in turn collected most of the learned and athletic honours and awards that the Royal Grammar School at Newcastle had to offer, he went South to Cambridge for his degree, instead of Edinburgh as hitherto and stayed in the South to earn a living as a headmaster. William became a minister and his son Denys, Professor of Medieval History at the old University of Edinburgh. For the rest, we have all drifted away from the land and from the countryside that gave us birth and direction. We are severally, lawyers, soldiers, schoolmasters, engineers, parsons, professors, musicians and even a lone airman. I suppose in the modern world of fast communications it was bound to happen but it hardly seems two hundred years ago that great great grandfather James looked across the home acres of Fishwick Mains and the waters of Tweed to the 'Muckle Cheviot' where his young son Alexander was learning his first trade of shepherding.

CHAPTER V

HEYDAY OF THE FIFIES, SKAFFIES AND ZULUS

And now as I take over the story and set down a few of my own most vivid recollections of the Bamburgh area of Northumberland just before the first World War, I find they are an odd mixture. They are of wind, and especially the biting cold of the January North Easters; but then they are also of peace and quiet trout streams between Great Moor and Cold Law, and of curlews calling across the moorlands in early spring. The memories should, I suppose, be of faces and of voices of people but I think they come into the landscape a little later. The rooks in the trees on the green at Bamburgh come first to mind and it is pleasant to find they are still in evidence when I pay far too infrequent return visits to it. Equally clear is a harsher but infinitely more evocative voice — the noise of the sheaves and pulley blocks of the zulus and skaffies of the Sea Houses fishing fleet stowing sail and unloading their catches in great baskets before drying out alongside the quay. The home coming of an engineless sailing fleet on a stormy evening, was something no small boy perched on the very outer end of the white washed pier below the great white revolving arms of the lighthouse could possibly forget.

Then, up behind, were the great smoke filled caverns of Uncle John's kipper yard with a great stir of barrels being trundled to and fro and mountainous stacks of freshly crated fish ready to be taken by the special two van goods train of the day, on the little single tracked North Sunderland branch line to the main London North-Eastern railway at Chathill for distribution to towns all over the kingdom. I remember the rows of laughing, muscular women in their shiny black aprons and wooden clogs, gutting, scraping and spiking the herring to the accompaniment of a seemingly ceaseless flow of outrageous joking and chatter.

There were delightful visits, I remember, to the Mc-Adam brothers who had, apart from an almost sub-tropical garden behind ten foot high stone walls, a cistern cut into the solid rock (it is said by the Romans who had a villa nearby). The outlet channel was so placed that sea water flowed in at high tide and changed the pool water in which cod and bass and all sorts of sea fish had grown to quite fantastic sizes over long years of feeding.

The great moment was when one of the elderly brothers would take us down the stone steps cut in the cliff to the edge of the pool and then call up his favourite fish by name to be fed. Later, I'm afraid we knew better, though at that age, it seemed simple magic — but I think we were rather unsophisticated children and none the worse for that.

So, one way and another, the sea filled a large part of our life in Bamburgh and Sea Houses. The rest of the time we looked across to the 'Muckle Cheviot' and explored further afield as we grew older.

But even at an early age I was taken for walks to places of mystery with dark sounding names like Glororum (Glower o'er 'em) I was told, but I find the Oxford Dictionary of Place Names sensibly keeps very quiet about it. Like all good Borderers, I was of course brought up on and remember with an illogical affection, the Laidly Worm (Loathsome Serpent) of Spindleston Heugh which is also a mile or so from Bamburgh. I suppose now-a-days she would have been called Ichthyosaurus and put in a museum and been totally 'unmemorable.'

I was fascinated by the beastie and often looked at the cliff in passing, though I am afraid the cave where the worm lived and the trough where she did 'sup the milk of seven stately cows' was made into a quarry fifty years before my time.

The legend observes most of the usual niceties. For those unlucky enough not to be raised in Northumbria, I had better explain. The fair Princess Margaret of Bamburgh Castle was turned into a dragon — the Laidly Worm —by her wicked stepmother who was, as usual, jealous of her beauty. The whole district was terrorised and had to feed her and bring the milk of these seven cows and pour it into a trough. Word went out that this would rapidly,

'Ruin the North Countree.'

In due time her brother, the Childy Wynd, heard tell and collected some buddies. They built a ship with — and this was the really clever bit —

'masts and spars of Rowan tree and fluttering silk so fine.'

Now, any respectable Northumbrian knows perfectly well that witches have no power over Rowan wood and the stepmother was a Northumbrian born and bred.

Nevertheless she sent her witch wives armed with the most powerful spells she could think up to destroy it. They failed miserably. Whereupon Childy Wynd landed in Budle Bay just to the North and, having carefully mugged up the proper drill,

'When he met the Worm
He sheathed his sword and bent his brow
And gave her kisses three;
She crept into the hole a worm
And stepped out a Ladye.'

So he 'wrapped her in his mantle,' not unnaturally, and took her home to King Ida's Castle, where equally naturally, the Queen it is said 'turned pale.' Anyway she was turned into a toad by the administering of three drops from the well — which gives one to think. The ballad adds,

'The virgins all of Bamburgh town
Will swear that they have seen
This spiteful toad of monstrous size
Whilst walking on the green.'

You can feel grateful that I have spared you the other thirty-seven verses! The song is about seven hundred years old and was written by a very famous old character, Duncan Frazier, who lived on the Muckle Cheviot and composed it from an ancient manuscript in 1270. And indeed, there is a road, or perhaps more accurately a narrow lane called the Wynd, in Bamburgh to this day.

More to the point, the whinstone pillars at Spindlestone to which the brother hitched the reins of his horse, is still there, surrounded to my mind by some of the most delightful country. To the North are the lonely sands of Budle Bay, with their razor shells and occasional fishing boats, and streams winding irresolutely across them. A little further on, opposite Holy Island, are the Beal Sands where the Celtic King Urien was betrayed and killed when almost within sight of wresting Bernicia from Ida's son.

Inland lies Chillingham and Wooler, with the swollen rills tumbling down Cheviot and setting out to wander across the lowland strip of the coast. I should go there in June, if you can, when the broom is in full splendour and clinging in a long trail of gold to the brown hillsides. There is gorse too and the Rowan will soon be out. Down from Cheviot itself runs the pleasant College Water. It starts in a place called the Henhole, with cliffs of 200 feet or so. Folk used to be attracted by seductive music coming from the ravine and quite a number, including a very merry hunting party some years ago went in and never came out. So watch it!

The Northumbrian hills are not spectacular, or high, or even rugged but they are blue and brown and seem to hang in the morning air as if piled up against the Western sky by some careless giant. Perhaps their greatest attraction is that they are covered with miniature denes, gullies to those from the South. You are always going round corners that break up what might otherwise seem a little round and dull for walking. They have in fact what every really memorable garden has, the element of surprise. I would add that they are pockety and snug, as are the little villages and market towns that nestle in the valleys or cling to the sheltered slopes.

The trout rivers we have already noticed. I soon added a rod and a tin of worms to my equipment and, ever optimistic, would take a pan so that I could fry them in butter. By nine I was still using worms, the luscious red 'branlings' that are found by digging out ripe manure heaps behind the farm. Even so, one had to keep out of sight, back from the banks because, if the fish saw you, it was all up in that pool. I would drop the worm into the water at the foot of a miniature waterfall and let it drift downstream and perhaps away round a bend into the next pool, until there was a slight tug on it which one hoped was a small trout which could be swung overhead on to the bank. If it came off it was sometimes impossible to find in the heather or long bents.

In some streams fish would be up to half a pound and have to be dragged, I'm afraid rather unprofessionally, ashore. But I have had as many as a couple of dozen good fellows, all waiting to be fried in oatmeal and butter. Later on in school holidays, the postman who cycled six miles up the valley to deliver mail in tin boxes in the dry stone walls for the remote farms, blowing his whistle to mark his arrival, would give me lessons in fly fishing. He was a past master at the art. He fished afternoons if the weather was suitable and the water peaty, and cycled back in the early evening with his catch and the outgoing mail.

I was I am sure, ill equipped for fly fishing of any sort. My rod was an old cheap stiff piece of cane, my reel and line of equally uncertain origin and the gut could be seen for miles in small pools and bright weather by the most myopic fish but I became reasonably proficient and soon used to join my mother, who was the keen fisherman of the family, in expeditions to the more remote haunts. I suppose the charm of fishing is that you are

pitting your wits against one of the most illusive preys
imaginable and success depends on subtle variants of light
and shade, sufficient wind to ruffle the water but not to
disturb the fish and perhaps a peat colour to cloud their
vision. I don't know. I never had time or opportunity
later in life to become really proficient.

I still cannot decide which is the best time for up-
country fishing. I loved the early moorland mornings just
before dawn when one could feel the whole world waking
up, the uncertain breeze in the burnside birches, rustling
in the heather and the first clear call of the curlew. The
hills were cool and fresh and a sort of light pre-dawn
grey glow would be spreading down the higher slopes of
the hills. Then the black summits would intensify just
before the sun burst over them and shot across the golden
fields far below in the Tweed Valley.

I think on the whole, I preferred the late evening
especially in autumn. After the restraint of the day, the
whole gamut of colours of the rainbow seemed to be
released in a way that flashes through the middle years
to light old age more vividly than any other memory.
The world runs riot and the birds sing with a sort of
conviction which is somehow lacking in the dawn chorus.
The trout seem more eager for their evening meal and,
if one is lucky, they can be cooked behind a wall or rock
shelter after dark and eaten, as they should be, under
a clear sky. Then we would wriggle into our waterproof
homemade sleeping bags. And tomorrow, perhaps there
would be another awakening before the magical hour of
dawn among the high glens.

I know there is another side of the coin. The coastal
strip is fairly dry but, my whiskers, it could be windy
and cold, especially when we had bathing parties at Easter!
I could add the lime kilns at Sea Houses if the wind was
in the wrong direction; this was the other main industry.
But this is a book for your enjoyment, so we will stick
to the facts that are fun and also, at least of passing

F

interest. In any case one simply doesn't remember the little unpleasantnesses a long time afterwards and in that, is perhaps the greatest dispensation of the Almighty.

What I cannot help recalling, are the journeys to the Holy Island, to the Lindisfarne of St Aidan and St Cuthbert with its history of early religious settlement and subsequent Danish raids. All in all it is perhaps best remembered as the home of the world famous Lindisfarne

Sunset — on the old way across the sands to Holy Island

gospels, the most beautiful illuminated manuscripts we have in which Celtic tradition is enhanced by Anglo-Saxon art at its best.

In those last few years of the Edwardian era of peace and established order of an apparently unshakeable society I was too young to think of these things however. I was much more excited about the drive across the flooded sands in the gig — we went everywhere by trap, gig or phaeton in those days when motor cars were still an unreliable rarity enjoyed by the rich. It is of course an island only at half tide. At low water you can drive across the muddy sands along a route which is marked by withies or poles. For those caught by the tide there were, if I remember rightly, two boxes on poles, one third and two thirds of the way across. But as these looked as if they would only hold about three people at a pinch it engendered some speculation as to what was supposed to happen to the rest and there seemed to be no provision at all for the poor horse. On a wild blustery day with the rain driving horizontally and the tide lapping in over the sands at a rate of knots, it could be a dauntting passage. Nowadays the track has been surfaced and one whizzes across by car in a few minutes.

In my young days the passage was made at a walking pace as the soggy sands precluded the horse dragging the dog cart any faster and it became a race with the tide, especially if one had miscalculated the hour of departure. On trips when the sea was breaking heavily on the Northern opening of the passage you would see a gaunt wreck of a brig sticking up starkly against the sky.

The wonderful ruins of the priory and the Norman parish church of St. Mary not to mention the nine inns (for a population of 908 of all ages) have been exhaustively written up in a great number of guide books to which I can safely commend you. To me, the rainbow arch is only memorable as being a suitable object at which to point my first little box camera with a fixed aperture and one forward speed. The camera had great advantages as it was strong enough to sit on when sandwich time came round. One thing I do remember, the wild flowers, especially the mallows, ragwort, restharrow and ladies bedstraw were a riot of colour and the little loch was an enchanted place of water birds and marsh flowers.

The castle was built as late as 1550 as a coastal fort and had then just been restored by Sir Edward Lutyens. From the Batteries you get a magnificent view of Berwick and St. Abbs Head to the North, the Farne Islands of course and all the heights of Cheviot. St Abbs Head brings back memories of the lonely stronghold of the 'Master of Ravenswood' and 'Caleb Balderstone.' In the days when it was really needed, that is when the Danes were sacking the Lindisfarne Priory and doing the monks a lot of no good, the castle didn't exist. When it was finally built in the 16th century as a coastal fortress, it was too late and, indeed, the only time it was ever attacked or captured was in the 'fifteen' rising by an enthusiastic Jacobite called Lancelot Ewington and his young nephew.

There was a government garrison at that time of fifteen, twelve of which Ewington invited to a party on board his little ship anchored in the bay below. When they were well filled and 'nicely thank you' he and his nephew entered the castle, pistols in hand and set about the other three soldiers, finally turning them out of the castle. Then they prepared the place for a siege, having first hoisted the white flag of the Pretender to the mast-head. The occupation only lasted two days, you will be sad to hear. After that a posse from Berwick came to the aid of the fifteen soldiers and together they re-possessed themselves of the castle in the name of the government. I can report that the gallant skipper got away eventually and after a necessary spell in France returned to Newcastle to run a pub for thirty years. He remained an uncompromising Jacobite to the end.

The most famous Bishop of Lindisfarne, St Cuthbert, the shepherd from the banks and moorlands of Tweed, who lived for many years as a hermit on the (then supposedly) devil haunted rocks of the Inner Farne Island is also too well documented to need a recapitulation here. But what, ever since boyhood, has intrigued me more than the pilgrimage of his life, is the really extraordinary wanderings of his body after death, when the devoted monks carried him from place to place for many long years to save it from pillage and robbery.

It must be remembered that in those days the Christian's body had far more significance and need of care by devoted followers than in these days when it has ceased to be of any use to its owner, or interest to anyone else, after death.

You will perhaps remember St Cuthbert had been at last persuaded by King Eagfrith and Archbishop Trumen, who came in person with a great following by sea to the hermit's cell on the Farne Island, to relinquish his solitary life of prayer and hardship on his rock and become Bishop of Lindisfarne. But, as he said, 'sickness and self mortification were already bringing him close to the Great Shadow.' In two years he was back in the cold stone cell on the Farne, having told a monk who asked when he would return,

'When you bring my body hither.'

A few weeks afterwards the body was brought back to Lindisfarne, and was put reverently in a large stone coffin and placed by the monks in the little Island Church of St. Peter. There, amidst the wild flowers and calling of the seabirds and chanting of the monks the Saint was allowed to rest in peace for nine years, the most cherished possession of the monks of the Priory. it has always seemed to me such an irony that only after death was his body, which during life was happy in a homespun undyed woollen habit, skin leggings and boots which were never removed from one year's end to another, wrapped in the most magnificent and costly vestments of purple and gold.

The coffin was opened for this to be done and so that the body could be put in a smaller coffin in case of need. But the body and clothes were found to be unchanged and flexible as in life. So back he had to go into the old stone box. In 793 back also came the Danes, sacking, burning and levelled most of Holy Island as was their wont but somehow they missed St Cuthbert's coffin. After that, when they next re-appeared in force in 875, the monks were taking no chances and popped their ex-Bishop into a much lighter portable wooden coffin as a temporary measure.

Now began one of the most remarkable treks in history. Off they went across the sands at a rate of knots to the mainland just ahead of the first wave of Danes.

They took also, fortunately for posterity, the famous Lindisfarne gospels.

The little party made their way across England, narrowly escaping robbers and marauding bands more than once. The idea was to get St Cuthbert across the sea safely to Ireland where there were many Celtic monasteries to give him a temporary resting place until it was safe to go back East. They got to the Cumberland coast just about where the old Roman fort of Ravenglass was still doing duty as a fishing harbour. They organised a boat and set sail for Ireland but their luck was out for the moment, as they ran slap into a great storm, during which they managed to hang on to the Saint but lost the gospels overboard. However, in these days of miraculous happenings you will not be surprised to hear they were washed up again safely on the shore, so all was well.

By that time, not surprisingly, they had had enough of the sea, especially in a small open boat and had wisely decided to stay firmly on land. There they remained for many years, leading a sort of wandering ecclesiastical life complete with St Cuthbert in his box and the priceless illuminated gospel manuscripts. It says much for the integrity of the monks at the numerous monasteries in which they lodged temporarily, that nothing was stolen.

The years went by and as all good journeys must come to an end some time, the monks decided on Chester-le-Street, for some reason which has been lost in the limbo of time. There St Cuthbert rested for a hundred years until the Danes, having made a meal of most of the coastal towns started to push inland. Up went the poor Saint in his little (temporary!) wooden box on to another pony's back and off the monks, or I suppose their successors, went. This time it was Southwards, over the Yorkshire moors and into the Pennines to the great monastery and Cathedral at Ripon.

They rested for a few months and, as all seemed quiet again on the East coast, they packed up St Cuthbert and the gospels once more and set off back for Chester-le-Street. But they never got there. I don't know how many of you recall the cow image carved on the main entrance to Durham Cathedral. Well, there is one and it commemorates the next incident. The little band were journeying along just South of Durham when they had a vision. And there, in the vision the saint himself gave them the direction they were to go. They were to follow a cow — which incidentally had just wandered into the picture — wherever it led them, until it stopped. Where it lay down to rest, there would be their abiding place. This they did and where the cow stopped eventually, they placed the Saint's coffin and built a little sort of chapel of boughs over him.

As soon as it became feasible they built a wooden temple round the coffin and found lodgings nearby. On September 4th 998 the saint was again removed, this time to Ealdhun's stone church. The body was allowed to rest there in peace until in 1069 William the Conqueror — not the Danes this time— swept through Northumbria to avenge De Comyn, laying waste the land as he went and slaughtering such a great proportion of the population that for ten years vast districts remained empty.

The monks' early warning system seems to have been working well and they departed by night with St Cuthbert and the gospels; no peace, even for the saintly! They fled back to their old Priory of Lindisfarne where they felt he would be safe as anywhere on the Holy Island, cut off from the mainland except at low tide. They hid his remains for a full year at Lindisfarne and then, as peace really seemed assured for at least the time being, the coffin was brought out of its secure hiding place and taken, still by the monks, back to Durham. There St Cuthbert found, you will be glad to hear, a final and peaceful resting place in the new church built by Bishop William. He is still there but I can't think, if there is indeed any continuity beyond the moment of death, that he is really happy about the arrangement. A grand cathedral was never his way of life and it might have been kinder to let him rest quietly on the one little wind-swept island that he had made his own.

It is now time to wind up the first conscious memories of youth in the land which has always generated a greater impression of colour and romance than any of the exciting foreign countries my wandering life as an airman has decreed that I should enjoy. That is, if I dare use that much abused word in its pre-film, Chaucerian sense. The past plays, perhaps a disproportionate part, in a boy's memories of the way he has travelled but I think this is as it should be. An affection for the past leads to a greater tolerance of the present, even when it is at its most daunting and in the contemplation of the beginning lies the surest hope of finding the most rewarding path-way into the future; are not bondage and expectancy the twin graces of childhood and the first faltering steps towards Bishop Gore's 'whole man?'

A corner of Sea Houses harbour
at the turn of the century

Thus my early bondage was to the twin delights of Northumberland — the hills and the sea. Perhaps the sea came first, because I could escape down the cliff to the little harbour of Sea Houses some years before I was allowed to wander away alone over the Cheviots. So the early memories are of rope wheezing through pulley blocks as the baskets of fish were swung ashore on the quay; of winch ratchets clacking and roaring and seagulls wheeling and screaming round wooden mast heads, as I sat enthralled on the whitewashed harbour wall below the little pierhead lighthouse. At other times I remember seeing, from the ramparts of Bamburgh Castle, the whole of the Scottish fishing fleet becalmed on its journey South to Lowestoft. There they lay floating about like so many toy ducks at all angles and so close that you could have heaved a pebble from one on to the decks of its neighbour. They had red sails and would have made a painter's paradise.

To see the fishing fleet set out, in the days of sail, was an unforgettable sight. There were of course no engines in those days before the first world war. As soon as the tide served and there was enough depth of water in the little harbour, the men and boys would troop down singly or in groups from the terraced houses on the hill and prepare to put to sea. The homecoming was even more exciting. From our house up on the harbour cliff we could often see the whole fleet — small dots beyond the Farnes getting in their nets and, one by one, making sail for home, either because the catch had been good or because the storm cone had been raised on the shore semaphore.

Often it developed into a race, especially between the Elliots and the Armstrongs who were reputed to own the fastest boats and were fairly well matched. But how slowly they actually seemed to come from the distant horizon, especially if the wind fell away, or turned offshore. Eventually lug sails would be dropped just at the harbour entrance, leaving enough momentum to stem any tide and arrive at their own berth with all way off. It always seemed a miracle of estimation. I was soon to learn the hard way, that it was not far short of one.

These first years of the twentieth century were the great years for the herring on that part of the coast. Later, the fishing fleet was to dwindle and finally to leave altogether. First the zulus and larger fifies and the few remaining round stemmed Yorkshire billyboys went South and everywhere, engines were eventually installed in the remaining craft and they went further afield for fish, leaving the lobster pots and offshore flat fish and whiting for the smaller cobles.

The zulus were fascinating boats with their raked canoe sterns. In most other respects they were almost indistinguishable from a fifie. Both had pointed sterns but the fifie's post was upright. We had a few skaffies — boats which have now disappeared without trace. They were the only East coast boats I know ever to have had both raked stem and stern posts. Anyway these were all drifters and not trawlers which is why they stuck to the great unwieldy lug sail, long after all other boats of this size had turned over to the more manageable gaff rig. I remember their black sides and high, unstayed foremasts —unstayed, that was, except for the halyard of the dipping lug sail set on a short yard. The halyard was set up well to windward. Even their most devoted adherents couldn't have called the mizzen elegant, being a square-headed standing lug set on a mast with a very pronounced forward rake and lightly stayed.

Both the skaffies and zulus (so named because we happened to be having one of our Zulu wars at the time) were Norwegian types of boat and, indeed, the familiar Viking longships of our history books had the same straight keels and overhanging ends, and were similarly, clinker built, though the bigger modern boats have become too heavy and beamy to row. The zulu was, in fact, an attempt by a cunning old fisherman in 1878 to build a boat combining the best features of both the skaffie and the fifie. The deep fore foot of the fifie, longer keel and finer bow was said to give her a better grip of the water when close hauled in a steep head sea and less tendency to broach-to when running. The raking ends of the skaffie were, on the other hand, said to make her a drier boat and she was certainly handier when going about. Arguments in the little Sea Houses inns were never ending and the coming of the zulu really settled nothing because it never did oust the two older types.

The Northumbrian coble is also a type all of its own. The broad planks, bold stern and high raking stern may originally have drifted across from Norway but the shingle beaches and lack of deep water harbours of the Northumbrian coast have determined her unique and quite odd characteristics. She has much deeper draught at the bow to enable her to grip the water and a flat shallow stern with two skorvels, or runners, which act as bilge keels when she is beached — always stern first. The rudder is, of course, unshipped earlier. At sea its great depth acts as a centreboard when beating. The rig is a simple dipping lug, flat headed and cut high in the clew, with bow lines to keep it taught in a wind. A curious feature is that, as the mainsail is reefed, the rake of the mast is increased, which brings the effective area of the sail amidships, by the time full reefing is reached.

For her size the coble is fast and she can stand up to really heavy seas (as I know to my cost!) but, oh boy, she requires expert handling, as she can broach-to with the greatest of ease when running and is extremely lively in a fresh breeze. But, for beach landing in heavy surf, she has no rival. The coble was supplied to East coast lighthouses during the nineteenth century; in fact it was a coble that Grace Darling and her father used to rescue the crew of the *Forfarshire* in one of the gales of 1838.

And to turn inland for one last look at the hills.

Clear and cool in the youthful mind's eye always is the Tweed which for excitement and wild loveliness is unrivalled. It is like a cottage garden of wild flowers which some countryman has charmed into life on the edge of the moors — moors which are in themselves a part of it. It is not unlike a child's idea of the landscape of the Pilgrim's Progress, a river winding through a mystical green country, with the Cheviots as the 'hilltops of the delectable mountains to cheer the pilgrim.'

Especially did it seem so on moonlight walks; not the mild moon of summer nights but the wild ice goddess of winter nights striding through the frozen sky trampling the scattered stars.

Perhaps the abiding memory is the view on an April morning from Cheviot, away Eastwards to where the mountain land breaks down into the narrow green strip of fertile land along the coast. There are green fields and the smoke of hearth fires and here and there a church nestling in the nook of a glen. There is the sound of running water nearby and the far off murmur of humanity. Beyond is the silver strip of the sea and the sun picking out the horizon. The morning wind blows as clean as the mid Atlantic and the air is full of the overpowering sweetness of fern, pine and bog asphodel; and there is the flash of trout rising in the nearby burn.

Half a century afterwards I can sit in the cockpit of our own little sloop in the quiet of the evening and recall the last shafts of light snaking out between the Sea Houses pier heads as those most beautiful of all sailing work boats came home to harbour. It is a pity that none of us will ever again see a big 70-foot Zulu under full sail, racing home with a catch — no wonder it is one of my most treasured early memories. (See illustration number 1).

These were, in their day, the largest luggers in Europe and with their going passed, not only an era of North Sea fishing, but a goodly portion of the light and colour of early 20th century Northumbria.

THE END

BOOKS FOR FURTHER READING

The Enchanting North, J. S. Fletcher (Eveleigh Nash, 1908)

The Farne Islands, F. Graham (1972)

The Lindisfarne Story, C. Cromarty (F. Graham)

The Romance of Northumberland, A. G. Bradley (Methuen)

The Violent Kingdom, Roy Anderson (F. Graham)

Anglo Saxon Northumbria, T. H. Rowland (F. Graham)

North Country Sketches, J. W. Allan (Courant Office, Newcastle on Tyne

Northumberland and the Border, W. White (Chapman and Hall, 1859)

Northumberland Yesterday and Today, Jean Terry (Andrew Reid and Coy.)

Bygone Northumberland, W. Andrews (W. Andrews & Co.)

Northumberland, W. Morris (Methuen, 1916)

Castles and Historic Homes of the Border, A. Eddington (Oliver & Boyd, 1926)

Wilson's Tales of the Border (Walter Scott, 1887)

Place Names of Northumberland, Mawer (C.U.P.)

Highways and Byways in Northumbria, P. A. Graham (MacMillan)

Highways and Byways in the Border, A. & J. Lang (MacMillan)

Northumberland, A. Mee (Hodder)

Northumberland East and West Borderland, Hill

Northumberland, Pevsner (Penguin)

A Northumbrian Remembers, Ridley Hall (County Hist. Reprint)

Northumbrian Wildlife, Balmain (F. Graham)

Northumberland and Scottish Border, Talbot (Methuen)

Northumberland County National Park — Countryside Commission (H.M.S.O.)

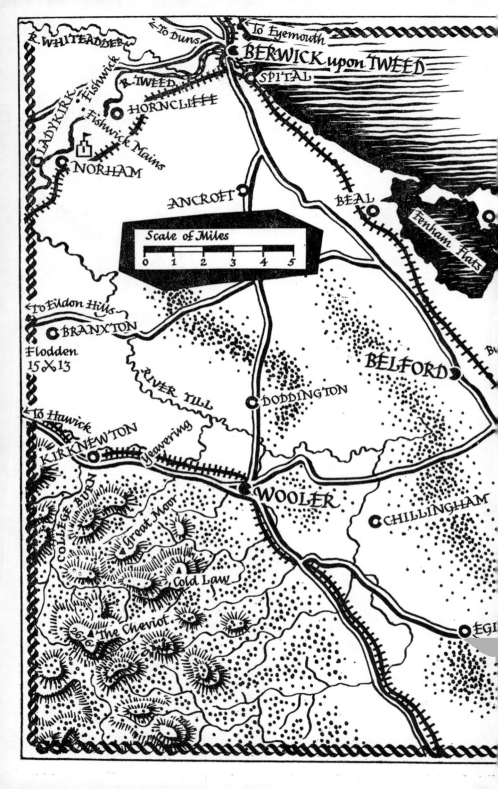